THE BERLIN WALL
and inner-German border
1945–1990

Wieland Führ

THE BERLIN WALL

WALL

and inner-German border
1945–1990

Michael Imhof Verlag

IMHOF-Zeitgeschichte

Title page:
Brandenburg Gate (Photo: Michael Imhof Verlag),
Inner-German border (Photo: Point Alpha),
Border guard Conrad Schumann jumping over the barbed wire to West
(Photo: ullstein bild – Peter Leibing)

Führ, Wieland: The Berlin Wall and inner-German border 1945–1990
(Imhof-Zeitgeschichte), Petersberg 2009

© 2009 Michael Imhof Verlag GmbH & Co. KG
   Stettiner Straße 25, D-36100 Petersberg
   Tel. 0661/9628286; Fax 0661/63686
   www.imhof-verlag.de

Design and reproduction: Michael Imhof Verlag
Translation: Michael Scuffil, Leverkusen
Printed by Fuldaer Verlagsanstalt, Fulda
Printed in EU

ISBN 978-3-86568-414-1

INDEX

Introduction 9

Germany and Berlin after World War II 1945–1949 13

Demarcation line, zonal borders and
inner-German border 1945–1952 29

Closure of the inner-German border –
Berlin as open city 1952–1961 38

13 August 1961 to 1989: The Berlin Wall and
reinforcement of the inner-German border 54

Over here and over there:
Travel and contacts in divided Germany 110

Flight, emigration and travel from East to West 144

The fall of the Wall and the end of the
inner-German border 1989/90 175

Literature 186

Museums and memorials 188

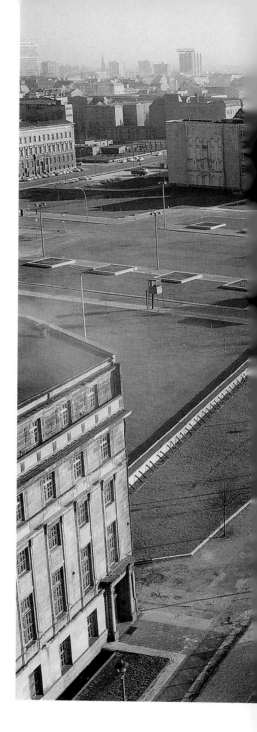

Brandenburg Gate (Brandenburger Tor) in Berlin with the border installations at the Berlin Wall, 1967 (Photo: Deutsche Fotothek)

INTRODUCTION

The border between the two Germanys arose as a result of the Second World War (1939–1945) unleashed by Nazi Germany. It had its roots in the intention of the victorious powers, and was laid down in the form of the planned occupation regime decided on by the United States, the Soviet Union and the United Kingdom at the Yalta Conference in the closing months of the war. After the unconditional German surrender and the takeover of government functions by the Allies, the four zones of occupation developed in different ways. The Soviet Union, which had occupied the eastern part of Germany and East Berlin, sought, by pressure and with the help of the "Socialist Unity Party of German" (Sozialistische Einheitspartei Deutschlands or SED), which was formed in 1946, to establish in its occupation zone the socialist system that already existed in its own state. When the German Democratic Republic (GDR, East Germany) was founded, this development was completed. The three Western powers (the USA, Britain and France) made possible the establishment of the other German state, the Federal Republic of Germany (FRG, West Germany) on a democratic foundation. When the two German states were integrated into the power blocs headed respectively by the USA and the USSR, West and East Germany found themselves at the focus of the Cold War and thus at the interface of systems in mutual opposition: economically, politically and militarily.

It was particularly the poor economic development, as well as the rigid political system imposed in the Soviet zone, that led to the departure, between the end of the war and the building of the Berlin Wall on 13 August 1961, of well over three million of its people for the West. While the borders between the three Western zones soon ceased to have any practical significance, the systematic entrenchment of the border between the Soviet zone and the Western zones, and later between East and West Germany and between East Germany and West Berlin increasingly became crucial instrument for the survival of the GDR leadership, supported and encouraged by the Soviet Union.

The borders between East and West Germany, and around West Berlin, developed from what had at first been a "green border", with relatively simple security, to become the most closely guarded and almost the most impenetrable border worldwide, comparable only to the still existing border between North and South Korea. In view of the increasing exodus of its own population and the imminent economic collapse of the country in 1960/61, the GDR regime ordered the hermetic sealing of the "Western border of the state" from 13 August 1961. According to East German propaganda, the "anti-Fascist protection wall" served the "maintenance of peace" and "protection from the class enemy". The form and function of the border installations made it clear from the outset, however, that they were directed inwards, against their own people. The sophisticated border technology, with its barbed wire, warning devices, walls and mined strips, was designed from the beginning to prevent escape from the GDR, the "Workers and Peasants' State". These border installations claimed numerous lives. The border, which divided two world systems, was monitored and administered by a huge state apparatus. The GDR budget for 1988 put aside more than 2.2 billion East German marks for the "protection of the state border". The GDR Ministry of State Security, which was largely involved in the border security system, had a separate budget of 3.6 billion marks. The amount allocated to all the GDR's universities and colleges in the same budget was 3.7 billion marks, while all areas of the arts together were assigned 2.9 billion marks.

The 1,393-kilometre border cut Germany in half. 155 kilometres of border surrounded West Berlin, of which 43 kilometres formed the border between the Soviet and Western sectors of the city. The Berlin border installations were particularly strongly fortified with concrete walls, hence the use of the term "Berlin Wall" as a synonym for the whole of the unnatural border through Germany. The dividing line between the two German states ran from Lübeck Bay southwards to the River Elbe, along the western border of Mecklenburg, through the Harz mountains and along the western edge of the Thuringian Forest before finally meeting the Czech border to the east of the town of Hof. The longest section of inner-German border, at 670 kilometres, was between Thuringia (or as it then was, the districts of Erfurt, Gera and Suhl) and the adjacent West German states of Bavaria and Hesse. For 45 years, the border divided geographical regions, towns and villages, disrupting roads and other communications, dividing families and friends, and leaving a permanent mark on the lives of millions of people. By sealing off the GDR in this unique manner, the regime succeeded in hugely restricting the escape of its own population to the West, thus for a time keeping the communist system alive. The border system, however, could not minimize the attraction exerted on large sections of the GDR population by the Western democracies and, in particular, by the living conditions in West Germany and West Berlin. On the contrary: the inaccessibility of a liberal democratic system with a considerably higher living standard lent a fascination to the West German state in particular, even though the image of a distant inaccessible world had a substantial admixture of illusion and wishful thinking. An authoritarian political system that often worked against the basic needs and rights of its own people led to increasing dissatisfaction within the GDR, whose political leadership was willing and able to make partial changes only to a minor degree and often only under the pressure of general international developments.

The changed political culture in the USSR, coupled with the economic decline of the communist superpower in the late 1980s, led not only to huge changes within the communist states of Eastern Europe, but ultimately had crucial implications for the existence of the GDR and not least for the border system. Occupations of West German embassies by East German citizens, a flood of applications for exit visas and moves to "the West", permeable borders in Czechoslovakia and Hungary, along with a vehement debate on the part of sections of the GDR public concerning the legitimacy of the leadership, and finally the "Monday demonstrations" in Leipzig and other East German towns and cities ushered in a process that was to lead to the fall of the Berlin Wall and the end of the inner-German border. 9 November 1989 marked the beginning of the end when the border was opened, an end which was consummated with the union of the two German states on 3 October the following year.

GERMANY AND BERLIN AFTER WORLD WAR II 1945–1949

Following the end of the Second World War in Europe on 8/9 May 1945 with the unconditional surrender of the German Reich, Germany, with its capital Berlin, was in a state of total devastation in every respect. The war had cost the lives of well over 50 million people worldwide. Hundreds of thousands of German soldiers were prisoners-of-war of the Allies. Many millions of Germans had lost their homes and all their possessions. Well over 12 million Germans fled from advancing Allied troops, and many did not return to their home region. Numerous German cities, such as Hamburg, Breslau (now Wroclaw), Nuremberg, Dresden and Berlin were nothing but ruins, all infrastructure having been destroyed. Industry and agriculture had seized up almost entirely, many people were starving. The most atrocious war in human history, unleashed by an unscrupulous German dictatorship, had come back with full force to destroy its instigators.

The first course for a post-war order in Germany had been set as early as 12 September 1944 by the three-power London Protocol. The European Advisory Commission (EAC), consisting of delegates of the three war Allies, had laid down that Germany was to be "divided into three zones for occupation purposes, each to be allocated to one of the three powers, and into the special area of Berlin, which is to be placed under an occupation authority of the three powers." Among the provisions of this Agreement was that Greater Berlin in the borders of 1920 was to be administered by an authority formed by the USSR, the USA and Great Britain. At the Yalta Conference in February 1945 Josef Stalin (1879–1953), Winston Churchill (1874–1965) and Franklin D. Roosevelt (1882–1945) decided to allocate to France, too, a zone of occupation and a sector in Berlin. There was no mention of a future division of Germany or of Berlin. After large parts of Germany had already been occupied by Allied troops, with fighting still going on in just a few territories and in the capital, the Soviet general Nikolai Berzarin (1904–1945) assumed command in Berlin on 28 April 1945 and on 14 May 1945 the city's first civil administration was appointed, with Dr Arthur Werner (1877–1967) as mayor. Even before the end of 1944 Aachen had become the first city to be liberated, having been occupied by the Americans, and it had been able to set up a provisional self-administration. The military advances by the Allied armies into German territory by the end of the war did not always match the politically planned zones of occupation, so that in July 1945, in accordance with the international agreements, the Americans and British withdrew from the territory they had temporarily occupied in Thuringia, Saxony, Saxony-Anhalt, Brandenburg and Mecklenburg, while Soviet forces handed over the western part of Berlin to American, British and French units, at the same time occupying the territories in eastern Germany allocated to them. Within the Western zones too there were adjustments in the occupation regime. During the first few months following the end of the war, the occupying powers took the chance to requisition whole industrial plants, vehicles, valuable commercial documents, cultural assets, and, not least, human resources in particular in the sphere of research and industry. These requisitions were understood as reparations.

Laboriously, life in the occupation zones and in Berlin began to return to normal in the months after the end of the war, though for a long time it seemed to be bare-

Signposts in Russian, Berlin, Wedding district, corner of Reinickendorfer Strasse and Paukstrasse, 1945 (Photo: Landesarchiv Berlin/ Otto Martens)

ly structured chaos. Most people's everyday lives were determined by the struggle for daily bread, worry about close relatives, friends and acquaintances, and fear of what each new day might bring. There was no time for reflexion on guilt or making amends. Psychological repression of the period so recently experienced served the interests of survival, and alongside the spiritual ruins it was above all the material ruins that had to be cleared away.

"An hour on Alexanderplatz. Watched the young gangsters and prostitutes. Bargaining; a Threepenny Opera without the songs. Then to the Brandenburg Gate. Alone. Occasionally you trip over a tramline; ... silence like in the mountains, only without the splashing of a glacial stream. In the newspaper there's a column devoted to the daily muggings; occasionally they find a naked corpse, and the murderers always come from the other side. ... Whole neighbourhoods without any light at all. Impossible to estimate the amount of rubble; but

as to the question of what is to happen to it, people simply ignore it by familiarity. A landscape of brick mounds, with people buried beneath them and stars above them, and the last creatures to move are the rats. ... A hundred paces further on are the women of the rubble, exhausting themselves with their buckets and shovels in an attempt to combat the unforeseeable; ... what remains of Berlin is the fame that hovers over certain locations, and the underground railway, which links these locations together. And in between, the gaping question of what really is."

Max Frisch (1911–1991)

On 11 July 1945 the Allied powers inaugurated the joint Control Council in Berlin. Stalin, Harry S. Truman (1884–1972), who had succeeded Roosevelt as US president on the latter's death in April, and Churchill (replaced halfway through the conference by Clement Attlee (1883–1967) following the British general election) met in the Cecilienhof, the former official residence of the Prussian crown prince in Potsdam. The fourth future occupation power, France, was not invited. The signing of the "Potsdam Agreement" by the three Allies on 2 August 1945 was the foundation of the post-war order in Germany, and also provided for major changes to the borders not only of Germany (in the east) but also of Czechoslovakia, Poland, Hungary and Romania. The Potsdam Agreement was thus also the basis not only of the expulsion of more than 12 million Germans from their homes, but also of the forced resettlement of hundreds of thousands of Poles, Ukrainians and other eastern European population groups. The Potsdam Protocol, to which France acceded on 4 August 1945, established the Allies' goals, which included the demilitarization, denazification, democratization and decentralization of Germany. However Germany continued to be regarded in the Protocol as an economic unit.

Anti-war poster, 1945, Berlin, Wedding district, Reinickendorfer Strasse 4 (Photo: Landesarchiv Berlin)

The authors of the text soon noticed that they had different interpretations of various terms. In particular the USSR on the one hand and the Western Allies on the other accused each other of not properly abiding by the Agreement. Even so, the jointly drawn-up constitution for Berlin came into force on 20 October 1945, and the same day saw the election of the city councillors and the members of the district assemblies. Voter turnout was 92%. The union of Social Democrats and Communists formed in the Soviet sector attained a share of 19.8% of the votes city-wide, and remained a minority even in the Soviet sector.

Even before the decisions taken at Potsdam, the Soviet military administration (SMAD) had allowed the formation of political parties in its zone of occupation with Order No. 2 of 10 June 1945. Alongside the Communist Party of Germany (KPD) and the Social Democratic Party of Germany (SPD), there were also two middle-class parties in the east of Germany, the Christian Democratic Union (CDU) and the Liberal Democratic Party (LDP). In mid-July 1945 these four parties in the Soviet zone combined to form the

Aerial photo of Dresden in ruins, 1945 (Photo:Sächsische Landes-, Staats- und Universitätsbibliothek Dresden, Deutsche Fotothek)

"United Front of anti-Fascist Democratic Parties", with the aim "of solving the great problems with united strength". The decisions of this so-called "Antifa Block" could only be taken with the unanimous approval of all four parties. The Soviet authorities however made no secret of their preference for the KPD, whose new leadership had not only been previously trained in the USSR, but had been appointed to important posts in the Soviet zone at the end of the war. The Soviet regime hoped that by quickly approving political parties under their influence as occupying

power, they would be able to transfer their system to the Western zones. In the back of their minds was the notion that the result of the dreadful war would lead to a massive shift to the left in all parts of Germany. From 27 July 1945 various democratic parties were approved in the Western zones, at first at local district level only. The first free democratic local elections since 1933 took place on 20 January 1945 in the American zone.

Following the resolutions of the Potsdam Conference, the Soviet zone underwent a different development from the other three. In September 1945 the Soviet Military Administration ordered the first thoroughgoing restructuring in its zone of occupation. As a result of a "land reform", landowners with more than 100 hectares and former leading Nazis were expropriated without compensation. In October there followed an education reform, and finally, under the pretext of "expropriation of the war criminals" a process started which by 1948 had led to the nationalization of more than 10,000 businesses without compensation. It was this thoroughgoing wave of confiscation that was to provide the foundation of the future communist planned economy in the GDR. Realizing that the KPD could not beat the SPD, the Soviet authorities, giving massive support to the communists, forced through the union of the two parties on 21/22 April 1946 to form the Socialist Unity Party of Germany (Sozialistische Einheitspartei Deutschlands or SED). In the Western zones this union did not take place, and met with massive resistance. To start with, the two old parties were equally represented in the executive organs of the SED, and a slight majority of its members were drawn from the SPD. At the first, and until 1990 the last, post-war free and democratic elections in eastern Germany in autumn 1946, the new party won a narrow victory in Mecklenburg, Thuringia and Saxony with the help of the Union of Mutual Farmers' Aid (Vereinigung der gegenseitigen Bauernhilfe (VdgB)). The CDU and LDP won narrow victories in Brandenburg and Saxony-Anhalt.

Germany's fate however was decided at international level. The term "Iron Curtain", used by the former British prime minister Winston Churchill in 1945/46 as a metaphor for the sealing off from the West of an incipient Eastern bloc under the hegemony of the USSR, also characterizes the development in international politics between the end of the war in 1945 and the fall of the Wall in 1989. The USA with its Western European allies and the Soviet Union with the Eastern European states in its sphere of influence, including the Soviet zone of Germany, forced the development of two mutually opposed world systems. The years 1946/47 saw a change in the German policy of the USA, which had hitherto still been based on co-operation with the USSR: the new policy was one of containment. While one side sought to prevent the dictatorial "Sovietization" of eastern Europe, the other attacked the "enslavement of Europe by US imperialism". The development of the two power blocs was ultimately to lead to the division of Germany. The union of the British and American zones into a single economic area known as the Bizone on 1 January 1947 gave rise to fears in the USSR that the western part of Germany would drift off into the "capitalist camp". This seemed to raise a question-mark over one of the Soviet Union's important post-war goals: the creation of lasting security against possible aggression by Germany with its new allies. The prevention of Western integration and the concurrent expansion of its own communist system became the cornerstone of Soviet foreign policy in the post-war period. As early as the middle of 1947, a further deterioration in relations between East and West became apparent. This was due on the one hand to the failure by the fourth conference of foreign ministers of the victorious powers, held in Moscow in March/April 1947, to agree on the German question, and on the other to the Truman doctrine proclaimed by the US president on 12 March of that year. This declared that the United States would support "free peoples against the communist threat" and became the foundation of the North Atlantic Treaty Organization (NATO) formed on 25 July 1949. Following the break-off of negotiations by the USSR, Poland and Czechoslovakia, the aid and reconstruction programme proposed by US Secretary of State George L. Marshall (1880–1959), addressed to all the countries of Europe, was only taken up by the Western zones of Germany and the countries of Western Europe. The conference of the state premiers of the newly constituted states in all four occupation zones held in Munich at the beginning of June 1947 never got beyond procedural matters, and the participants from the Soviet zone left the conference table. By the start of 1948, a political process was taking shape which could only logically end in the formation of two German states. During the course of the year, the structures in the two halves of the country became further entrenched. The bizonal economic council, formed in Frankfurt am Main in May 1947, was accorded wide-ranging powers at the start of 1948, resembling in fact those of a parliament. The "German Economic Commission", formed in the Soviet zone likewise in 1947, was given legislative powers in February 1948, and thus became part of the institutional structure of an embryonic state. The six-power talks in London in February 1948 recommended the establishment of a West German government.

When the Berlin city council voted 89 to 17 to elect the Social Democrat Ernst Reuter (1889–1953) as mayor on 24 June 1947, the Soviet city commandant vetoed the decision and prevented him from being sworn in. In January 1948 the Soviet occupation authorities obstructed the land access routes to West Berlin. When the city council introduced a new constitution on 22 April 1948, the Soviet representatives once again objected. The Allied negotiations on a currency union covering the whole of Germany came to no conclusion, with the result that the Western powers carried out a currency reform of their own in the Western zones in June 1948. Thereupon the Soviet representatives walked out of the Allied Control Council in Berlin on 16 June 1948 and ordered stricter controls on all access routes to the city. The commander-in-chief of the Soviet forces in Germany im-

North Sea

Baltic Sea

Hamburg

Bremen (part
of the American
Occupation Zone)

Soviet
Occupation
Zone

British
Occupation
Zone

Potsdam Berlin

Cologne

Halle

Dresden

Frankfurt

French
Occupation
Zone

American
Occupation Zone

Stuttgart

French
Occupation
Zone

Munich

Germany after 8 May 1945 and the results of the Potsdam
Conference on 2 August 1945
dotted line = provisional demarcation line between the areas
occupied before 8 May 1945 by the Red Army in the east and the
US Army in the west

posed a currency reform of his own on the Berlin city
government, a move immediately declared null and
void by the Western Allies. Thereupon the Western
city commandants introduced the deutschmark, now
already the currency of the Western zones, to the
Western sectors of Berlin too. With a few days' delay,
the Soviet zone carried out a currency reform of its
own. Meanwhile events proceeded at a precipitate

pace. On 24 June 1948, the Soviet occupation forces cut off all overland access to West Berlin. Two days later, the Americans, with the strong support of the British, improvized an "airlift", for which all available transport aircraft were mobilized. The imposition of the blockade by the Soviet Union was an extreme measure. Hunger, unemployment and the economic collapse of West Berlin were part of the calculation. Supplies in the Western sectors of the city were sufficient for at most a month. The Soviet leader Josef Stalin could be certain that the Western powers would be unable to create a land corridor to the city, as to use force to do so would provoke a war. The American military governor in Germany, Lucius D. Clay (1897–1978), was determined to hold out. The number of transports deployed in the airlift increased constantly, reaching a peak on 15/16 April 1949 with 1,398 flights carrying 12,940 tons of supplies in 24 hours. All in all, the airlift consisted of 277,264 flights with a payload of 1,831,200 tons, which kept the Western sectors of the city alive. Known lovingly by the Berliners as "raisin bombers", the aircraft made a major contribution towards a change of attitude on the part of large sections of the people of West Berlin. In their distress, they developed feelings of comradeship and gratitude for the former enemies. This operation to defeat Stalin's blockade cost 39 British, 31 American and 8 German lives.

During the airlift, political relations between the Soviet sector and the Western sectors worsened still further. On 6 September 1948 communist demonstrators prevented a session of the Berlin city council in the Rotes Rathaus, its seat to date, which was in the Soviet sector. Subsequent sittings of the city council and government, which still acted on behalf of the whole city, were held in a district town hall, the Rathaus Schöneberg, which was later to become the headquarters of the West Berlin city government and

Unloading the "raisin bombers" at Tempelhof airfield during the Berlin Airlift in 1948, (Photo: U.S. Air Force)

mayor. The Soviet city commandant thereupon declared that the "Berlin city government and council had made themselves tools of the Anglo-American authorities, who were pursuing an anti-democratic division of Berlin." On 9 September Ernst Reuter called a protest rally outside the former Reichstag building. In spite of cold and rainy weather, it was one of the most impressive mass demonstrations ever held in the city. Ernst Reuter's appeal: "Peoples of the world, look at this city!" was the emotional climax of his speech to tens of thousands of Berliners.

On 30 November 1948, the "Democratic Block" met in the Admiralspalast in the Soviet sector and "in view of the fact that the government elected in 1946 has disregarded the most basic interests of Berlin and its people, and by constantly neglecting its duty has not fulfilled its obligations," elected a provisional "democratic city government". Friedrich (Fritz) Ebert (1894–1979), a son of the first president of the Weimar Republic Friedrich Ebert (1871–1925), was elected mayor of East Berlin. The twelve Western city districts thereupon held elections on 5 December 1948, in which 32 seats were reserved for the Soviet sector. Ernst Reuter was now able to take up his position as mayor in the Western sectors.

The Soviet Union finally ended its blockade of West Berlin on 12 May 1949. The division of the city had by now become a fact, and the cleft between the Western Allies and the Soviets had become immeasurably deeper. Both sides had institutionalized their positions, West Berlin had increasingly to accustom itself to an island existence. The policy of the USSR, namely to prevent a separate Western state in Germany, and thus the process of integrating the Western zones into the Western world, had in turn failed, but was still pursued with every means available.

After meetings of the committee to prepare a constitution had been held in the Western zones in 1948, and a Parliamentary Council formed under the chairmanship of Konrad Adenauer (1876–1967), the Basic Law of the future Federal Republic of Germany was drawn up. Accepted by the Parliamentary Council on 8 May 1949, it entered force on 23 May. Bonn had already been chosen as the provisional seat of government on 10 May. Free democratic elections for the first German Bundestag or parliament were held on 14 July 1949. Theodor Heuss (1884–1963) of the Free Democratic Party became the first president of the Federal Republic. On 15 September 1949 Konrad Adenauer (Christian Democratic Union) was elected Chancellor, and in his first government declaration when introducing his cabinet committed the Federal Republic to Western integration.

On 7 October 1949 the German Democratic Republic (GDR) was formed in the Soviet zone. The pseudo-democratic People's Council, which had been elected in May 1949 on the basis of single lists at the Third People's Congress in the Soviet zone, declared itself a Provisional "Volkskammer" ("People's Chamber"),

Blockade of the Western sectors of Berlin. Berliners watch as the aircraft fly in to Tempelhof airfield, 1948 (Photo: Landesarchiv Berlin)

or parliament. The SED leadership avoided a free democratic election because it was clear that they would lose a substantial share of the vote even relative to the previous democratic elections in the Soviet zone in 1946. Four days later, the Provisional Volkskammer elected Wilhelm Pieck (1876–1960) President and Otto Grotewohl (1894–1964) Prime Minister of the GDR. Both were members of the SED. Representatives of the other approved parties were enticed with the promise of government jobs. The capital of the GDR was East Berlin, later officially "Berlin, capital of the GDR". The division of Germany was now complete. Even though proposals for re-unification were made, from various motives, by both German states and by the four occupying powers, everyone was clear that this would not happen in the foreseeable future. The incipient "Cold War" between the two blocs, headed respectively by the USA and the USSR, both nuclear powers, was now to be played out first and foremost on German soil. While the formation of the Federal Republic was supported by large sections of the population, in the GDR it was only a minority that viewed the Sovietized communist system with any pleasure. As a result, the East German leadership was forced, if it wanted to retain power within the community of communist states under Soviet leadership, to secure itself primarily against opposition from within. After economic and other performance proved modest, when it became clear that far-reaching structural changes were impeding development in all areas in what was much the smaller of the two Germanys, and especially when it was obvious that the "other Germany" was making giant strides forwards, especially where the economy was concerned, it was not long after the foundation of the GDR that work started on what was, in Germany's history, a unique border system.

US Jeeps on patrol on the border between Hesse (US zone) and Thuringia (Soviet zone), c. 1949 (Photo: Point Alpha)

DEMARCATION LINE, ZONAL BORDERS AND INNER-GERMAN BORDER 1945–1952

The four zones were separated by demarcation lines laid down by the Allies as early as 1944 in the London Protocol. Essentially they followed the old provincial borders of Germany as of 1937. After the powers had definitively occupied the agreed zones of occupation in the first half of July 1945, a few adjustments were made, small areas of territory being exchanged between zones. These adjustments were mostly agreed by the senior military. One well-known example was the "Wanfried Agreement" between the American and Soviet forces. The US zone was basically in the south, but to give the Americans access to the sea, it also included the North Sea port of Bremerhaven with its associated (but separate) city of Bremen. Links between Bremen and the main US zone were dependent on a rail connection which in places in central Germany ran through Soviet-occupied territory. A few local authority areas in Hesse (in the US zone) were, in consequence, swapped for areas in neighbouring Thuringia (in the Soviet zone).

The course of the demarcation line between the Western zones on the one hand and the Soviet zone on the other was, to start with, marked by coloured posts and other signs on trees, and even these were not set up along the whole line. Roads that crossed between zones were in many cases closed by barriers, and here and there the first wire fences appeared, along with notices pointing to the existence and position of the demarcation line. There was still no comprehensive border security, and at this time the demarcation line was barely visible. Only the surveillance carried out under Directive no. 23 of the Allied Control Commission, originally carried out exclusively by soldiers of the occupying powers, gave any indication of the border between East and West, and thus between two increasingly different political systems.

Even in the immediate post-war period in 1945, crossing the demarcation line legally required Allied consent. In the autumn of that year, the Allied Control Commission issued the first regulations relating to inter-zonal movement of people and goods. In the con-

Zonal border control point at Glienicker Bridge on the road to Potsdam: East German border policeman and Soviet soldiers by their guardhouse, c. 1950 (Photo: ullstein bild)

Barrier near Asbach/Thuringia (East) on the border with Bavaria (West), 1950 (Photo: Bundesarchiv Koblenz/ADN ZB/Donath)

fusion of the times, none of these measures prevented hundreds of thousands of people from crossing the demarcation line without official consent. Their motives were various: men, women and children were searching for family and friends; those who had been bombed out or expelled from their homes were searching for a roof over their heads or a new home; refugees, released POWs and former forced labourers were on their way home, or to a new home. Those Germans who had remained in Czechoslovakia or in those areas in the east now occupied by Poland were systematically driven out.

Even in these early days, there was a massive movement of people towards the Western zones. A major role was played too by the smuggling of food, such as potatoes, butter and lard, and of simple everyday needs such as stockings, light-bulbs and razor-blades. Hoarding, and the black market across the still only loosely guarded border, developed for many people into a lucrative business. There were also border guides, who, for a fee, took people mostly from East to West, or others with an eye to business who exploited the distress of the times to smuggle difficult-to-come-by goods across the zonal borders on a grand scale. Sometimes Allied soldiers exploited these structures to their own advantage. Inns, mills and isolated, exposed farms close to the demarcation line were often the bases for these illegal border-crossers, blackmarketeers and smugglers. Most illegal border crossings were made at night. Those who were caught were often sent straight back to their zone and given a caution, but sometimes interrogated and their goods confiscated. In serious cases, especially of economic crime or suspected espionage, prison sentences were imposed. These measures were also applied in the Western zones. Occasionally the Allied border guards collaborated with the illegal border-crossers, turning a blind eye to their activities in return for a consideration. From time to time, though, Soviet soldiers would shoot at "border violators", and this resulted, particularly along the demarcation line between Thuringia (Soviet zone) and Bavaria (American zone), in the first fatal casualties of the inner-German border.

On 30 June 1946 the Allied Control Commission, at the request of the USSR and in agreement with the Western Allies, issued a decree to close the demarcation line. All four Allies had an interest in restricting what was proving to be a mass migration to the West. The Soviet authorities feared a loss of prestige and a loss of skilled workers. The three Western powers, by contrast, were faced by supply and accommodation problems posed by the ongoing stream of refugees into their own zones. From then on, the zonal borders could only be crossed with an inter-zonal travel permit, an inter-zonal passport or a migration permit. For people living in areas close to the demarcation line between East and West, there was a border ID for what was known as "local border traffic", the chief beneficiaries of which were those with jobs in the

Border between the American sector of Berlin and the Soviet zone, Lake Griebnitz, Berlin, Zehlendorf district, c. 1950 (Photo: Landesarchiv Berlin/Ewald Guilka)

West. The demarcation line could now be legally crossed only at a few defined points, which later became the border crossing-points. Responsibility for guarding the zonal borders, in particular the East/West border, was increasingly transferred to German authorities. The first to do so was the newly formed Customs Border Guard in Lower Saxony (in the British zone), which took over some areas of border surveillance as early as September 1945. The Hessian Border Police and the Bavarian Border Police (both in the US zone) were formed in May 1946 and on 15 November 1946 respectively. Three days later, the Soviet Military Administration ordered the setting up of a German Border Police (Deutsche Grenz-polizei – DGP) in its zone.

On 1 December 1946 the first border police units and border guards took up their posts in the East, at first only giving support to the Soviet border guards. Along the 2,236-kilometre land border of the Soviet zone (including the eastern and Czech borders) 2,543 guards were posted to start with, whose tasks included "the prevention of illegal border crossing, illegal trade, people-smuggling and gangsterism, the search for Nazi and war criminals, and illegal fascist and militarist groups and other lawbreakers, and above all the prevention of flight to the Western zones". The newly formed border-police units were originally a section of the regular police forces of the re-created states within the Soviet zone. Their structure at first varied considerably.

With its low manpower levels, inadequate training and poor equipment, the border police in the Soviet zone were hardly up to the job of guarding the border, and for a long time depended on the support of the Soviet military. The year 1947 saw an extensive re-organization of the German Border Police, with increased manning levels and simplification of its structure. They now all wore the same blue uniform and were equipped with old German ex-army K 98 carbines and pistols. Increasingly the developing division be-

The border village of Mödlareuth. The stream marks the zonal border between Thuringia and Bavaria, which ran thorough the middle of the village. July 1949 (Photo: Bundesarchiv Koblenz, ADN ZB/Donath

tween the Soviet zone and the Western zones was making itself felt among the general public in Germany. In November 1948, during the Berlin airlift and in connexion with the currency reform in Western Germany and the Western sectors of Berlin, the German Border Police was taken out of the control of the states in the Soviet zone and placed directly under the Border Police department of the German Interior Administration. Thus by the

West German border protection officers on duty, 1950s (Photo: Point Alpha)

end of 1948, the Soviet zone had a centrally managed, militarily organized special police formation. Even at this early date, the German Border Police had set up guard posts in a ring around Berlin, whose purpose was to restrict free access to the individual sectors. When the German Democratic Republic was founded on 7 October 1949, the border police department was renamed, becoming part of the "German People's Police" ("Deutsche Volkspolizei") department in the Ministry of the Interior. By now, the German Border Police had a strength of more than 20,000. In 1950, its responsibility was extended to securing the GDR sea border.

In West Germany, the Federal Border Protection Force (Bundesgrenzschutz or BGS) was not formed until 16 March 1951, being placed under the control of the Federal Ministry of the Interior. In co-operation with the Bavarian Border Police and the Customs Police, its particular task was to monitor and guard the borders with the GDR and Czechoslovakia, and to man the border crossing-points. The Federal Border Protection Force was organized at first into Border Protection Commands West (from 1953 Centre), North and South, each with four sections of 600 officers each, plus a Coastal Border Protection Unit (500 officers) and a Border Protection Unit (Buildings). The establishment was originally approximately 10,000, being raised to 20,000 as early as mid-1953. After various structural changes in the mid 1950s, and new equipment, e.g. the setting-up of an aerial capability in Hangelar, the second Federal Border Protection Force Law came into effect force on 31 May 1956. Its provisions included the transfer of some 9,600 BGS officers to the armed forces. These included the whole Coastal Border Protection Unit, which formed the nucleus of the Federal German navy.

By 1961, the strength of the BGS had been raised to 14,000 once more. Additional units were introduced, including pioneer and signals units. In mid 1961 the BGS was organized into four Border Protection Commands with four technical and four training departments, eight Border Protection Groups and 24 Border Protection Departments, plus the Border Protection Command (Schools), the Border Protection Passport Service and the Border Protection Administration. 1964 saw the formation of the Border Protection Aerial Group, which by 1970 had some 50 helicopters at its disposal. Also in 1964 the Border Protection Force (Marine) was reconstituted. From 1961/62 all the BGS Commands had Intelligence Centres to undertake reconnaissance and espionage tasks. These sent their information on to the reconnaissance and espionage units that existed in the federal states bordering on East Germany and Czechoslovakia.

Until 1952 there was still a certain degree of permeability in the East/West border system. However, a

Road block in Berlin, Charlottenstrasse, between Kreuzberg district (US sector) and Mitte district (Soviet sector) 8 August 1951. East Berlin calls itself the "democratic sector" (Photo: Landesarchiv Berlin/Gert Schütz)

further extension of the border installations, a tightening of bureaucracy in cross-border traffic and an increase in manning levels in the East German border police made it increasingly difficult to cross the inner-German border. Even by the end of 1949, the year the two German states were founded, the GDR border police in Thuringia had registered for its stretch of border that 193,186 people, overwhelmingly inhabitants of the Soviet zone or later the GDR, had been arrested, and that they had opened fire 6,506 times. These had mostly been warning shots, but 40 people had been wounded and twelve killed. The Thuringian border police noted "little activity on the part of the Western police".

CLOSURE OF THE INNER-GERMAN BORDER – BERLIN AS OPEN CITY 1952–1961

At the start of 1952 the Volkskammer (parliament) of the GDR passed a law approving all-German elections to a national assembly. However, the USSR and GDR had already dismissed any idea of these elections' being monitored by a commission of the United Nations, whereupon the federal government in Bonn rejected the conditions laid down by the East. The background was the so-called Stalin Note on the re-unification of Germany, sent by the Soviet leader to the Western powers: Stalin's proposal for a united Germany presupposed the country's neutrality.

With the conclusion of the German Treaty in Bonn on 26 May 1952, which accorded the Federal Republic equal status in the community of Western European nations, and the foundation of the European Defence Community in Paris the following day, the Western integration of the young Federal Republic entered a new phase. This also meant the definitive failure of Soviet plans to prevent just this. It was during the period when the German Treaty was being prepared with the three Western powers that the decisive preparations were made for sealing off the GDR from Western Germany by tightened border security.

On 5 May 1952 the leadership of the central border department of the (East) German Border Police were summoned to the Soviet Control Commission in the Karlshorst district of Berlin, at which a revision of the inner-German border regime was discussed. On 16 May 1952 the German Border Police was organizationally separated from the general police force, the

House in Thuringia (Buchmühle) on the border with Hesse, in the foreground the barbed-wire border fence, c. 1952 (Photo: Point Alpha)

Volkspolizei or "People's Police", and placed under the control of the East German Ministry of State Security, better known as the Stasi (Ministerium für Staatssicherheit – MfS). Finally, in direct collaboration between the ministry and the leadership of the SED, all the measures were taken that were necessary for the new border regime to be announced on the same day that the Federal Republic signed the German Treaty. At the same time, massive propaganda steps were taken to prepare the GDR population, especially those who lived close to the border with West Germany. Disinformation in the regional GDR press reported that the Federal Republic was planning police measures directed against the GDR and the people living near the border. In fact, ever since the East German state was founded, a major role had been played by ongoing attempts to stoke up the fear of "imperialist agents and saboteurs" who were allegedly seeking to disrupt the establishment of the GDR.

In the 1950s this artificially inflamed hysteria became an important component of political propaganda, which was also designed to distract attention from the GDR's political and economic failures. It was on the very day of the signature of the German Treaty, 26 May 1952, that the Council of Ministers of the GDR proclaimed the "Decree relating to measures on the Demarcation Line between the German Democratic Republic and the Western Zones of Occupation". The choice of language is not insignificant: the expression "demarcation line" was still used, rather than "state border", and while the GDR here in this important document of post-war history, and later, was extremely meticulous about using only the term "German Democratic Republic" (or the abbreviation GDR) for itself, in this important document the Federal Republic was called "the Western occupation zones". The "Police Decree regarding the Introduction of a Special Regime along the Demarcation Line" was issued the same day, and published the day after, i.e. on 27 May 1952: it laid down the regulations which in principle were to remain in force for the border zone of the GDR until 1989. From the point of view of the GDR, this decree provided the legal framework for the transformation of the demarcation line into a fortified and highly secure state border. The area close to the border was declared a restricted zone, in fact three zones of increasing restriction. At a stroke, it changed the lives of hundreds of thousands of people on both sides of the border, and in particular severely limited the freedom of movement of the 17 million inhabitants of the GDR. The decree was signed by Wilhelm Zaiser (1893–1958), the then Minister of State Security in the GDR, to whom the German Border Police was by now subordinated. Its sections read as follows:

1: The designated restricted zone along the demarcation line between the German Democratic Republic and

Forcible evacuation from the restricted zone in Thuringia, summer 1952 (Photo: Point Alpha)

West Germany [sic: Westdeutschland] shall comprise a control strip 10 m in width immediately adjoining the demarcation line, a protective strip approximately 500 m in width immediately on the demarcation line, and a restricted zone approximately 5 km in width.

2: The existing stipulations regulating local cross-border traffic are hereby revoked. The demarcation line may only be crossed at the designated control points with a valid inter-zonal pass.

3: With immediate effect, no inter-zonal passes will be issued to residents of the restricted zone. Residents of West Germany will no longer be issued with residence permits for the restricted zone. Entry to the restricted zone with an inter-zonal pass or visa is prohibited with immediate effect.

4: No person shall enter the 10 m control strip. Any person who shall attempt to cross the control strip towards either the German Democratic Republic or West Germany will be arrested by the border patrols. Non-compliance with the instructions of the border patrols will result in the use of weapons [by the patrols].

...

6: No public assembly, demonstration or mass event of any kind shall be held in the 5 km restricted zone without a permit. The permit shall be obtained through the local administrative organs from the responsible Border Police command 24 hours before the event is due to commence. All events, assemblies etc. shall finish by midnight.

...

8: Residents of the German Democratic Republic outside the restricted zone who for occupational or other reasons (e.g. official business, visiting relatives etc.) wish to enter the restricted zone temporarily shall apply to the district office of the Deutsche Volkspolizei in their place of residence for a pass to enter the 5 km restricted zone. Any person who thus temporarily enters the restricted zone shall within 12 hours report to the local police authorities, and again on leaving the area.

9: ... Members of the public shall immediately report to the German Border Police any person within the 500 m protective zone who is there illegally.

10: Within the 500 m protective zone no person shall be on the fields or roads, operate any kind of vehicle or perform work of any kind outside the home except between the hours of sunrise and sunset. Work in the immediate vicinity of the 10 m control strip shall only be performed under the supervision of the Border Police. Places of work outside of built-up areas shall be accessed using only those routes stipulated by the Border Police.

11: Public houses and restaurants, cinemas, boarding houses, recreational institutions and other places of public resort within the 500 m protective strip are hereby closed. Assemblies and mass events of any kind are prohibited.

...

13: ... No person shall have the right to enter the 500 m protective strip unless he or she is on a list maintained by the local border command. ...

From "Police Decree regarding the Introduction of a Special Regime along the Demarcation Line"

GDR, 26 May 1952

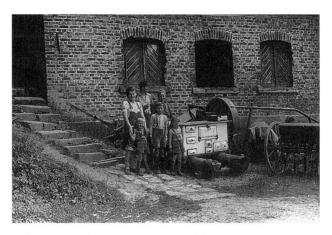

A family from Thuringia after a successful escape to Hesse, May 1952 (Photo: Point Alpha)

In connexion with the now totally changed situation, thousands of people in the area of the GDR bordering on the Federal Republic were compulsorily resettled in an unparalleled operation in the summer of 1952, often having to leave their home district, their friends and relations, and their belongings within 48 hours. By the autumn of 1952, more than 2,400 families comprising some 8,400 individuals had been compulsorily resettled away from the border zone of the GDR. Numerous people tried to protest against and resist this resettlement. In Thuringia they were supported by the leadership of the protestant church and in some cases by fellow citizens. The compulsory resettlement was carried out by the responsible state organs under the code name "Operation Vermin". Commissions were set up to establish who in the individual towns and villages was to be considered "politically unreliable" in the still young GDR. This involved arbitrary and subjective interference in the lives of many families. More than 6,400 people escaped these state-ordained compulsory measures by fleeing to the West. Including them, a total of about 15,000 people were directly affected by the compulsory resettlement.

Those removed from their home localities were accused, with or without evidence, of "Western contacts", a Nazi past, unwillingness to take part in what the GDR considered desirable social activities, criminal acts, or simply an anti-democratic attitude. Those thus compulsorily resettled felt that they had been branded in some way, and continued to feel that they were under surveillance by the "state organs" of the GDR. Few managed to return to their homes while the regime persisted. Only after the fall of the inner-German border on 9 November 1989 was it possible for most of them, after decades of compulsory resettlement, to return to their homes and, after lengthy legal proceedings, obtain restitution of their unlawfully confiscated property.

Some 400,000 inhabitants of the GDR remained in the newly formed restricted zone, and from then on suffered massive impairment of their quality of life through continual inspections and other state-imposed conditions. In the decades to come, the GDR leadership attempted to use tax relief and better provision of food and everyday necessities in order ease the situation for those remaining in the restricted zone. The accustomization process for those living in the border area was a lengthy process. In the 1950s and early 1960s, conversations and contacts between friends and relations across the barbed wire and other barriers was still possible; after all members of families thus torn apart often lived literally metres away from each other on either side of the border. Small gifts could be thrown across and children in the border villages would tease each other across the border, while riding their trikes across the freshly raked control strip. Fines and a stricter border regime increasingly prevented these contacts, and after the building of the Berlin Wall in 1961 and the consequent reinforcement of the inner-German border, they ceased altogether. By the end of August 1952, the 23 GDR border dis-

GDR border police ploughing the 10-metre control strip along the border between Thuringia and Hesse, after 1952 (Photo: Point Alpha)

tricts had spent more than five million East German marks on the measures required by the decree of 26 May 1952. For comparison, a teacher in the GDR earned about 200 marks a month at this time. More than half of the amount budgeted for the strengthening of the border, 2.7 million East German marks, was used to set up the 10-metre-broad control strip along the demarcation line, which was almost complete by the end of October 1952.

The regions close to the border on either side, which had grown together historically over the centuries, were now torn apart at a stroke. In East and West alike, this led to considerable economic problems. Factories lost their sources of supply, some of their employees, and, in many sectors, their customers too. Agricultural land and woodlands ceased to be viable, and the decline in agriculture in the border areas was aggravated as a result. While land in the East belonging to West German landholders was expropriated without compensation, and was later mostly incorporated into the collective farms known as "Agricultural Production Cooperatives" (German abbreviation LPG, for "Landwirtschaftliche Produktionsgenossenschaft"), West

German tenants of landlords in the East mostly paid their rent into an escrow account. As a result of ongoing nationalization, the planned economy and the consequent state regulation, GDR operations mostly had fewer problems with the drastic changes resulting from the abrupt closure of the border. Those East German workers who had jobs in the West (which paid better) were now faced with a choice, however: either to flee to West Germany, or to find new work in the GDR. In exceptional cases, a few West German workers were allowed, until the final sealing-off of the border with the building of the Berlin Wall in 1961, to continue working in the GDR close to the border, for example in the slate mines in Lehesten (Thuringia). Only in Berlin was it possible for inhabitants of the Western sectors to work in the East of the city without restriction, and vice versa, until August 1961.

People in the areas of West Germany bordering the GDR were faced with major problems as a result of the border closure. Already in the late 1940s, these regions had faced additional economic problems as a result of the arrival of migrants from eastern Germany

A patrol of the (East) German Border Police monitoring the banks of the River Elbe, 1956 (Photo: Bundesarchiv Koblenz, ZB)

Coastguard vessel of the (East) German Border Police off the island of Rügen, 14 December 1955 (Photo: Bundesarchiv Koblenz, ZB)

and other parts of eastern Europe. In largely agricultural regions, such as the Franconian areas of Bavaria, it had been hardly possible, even then, to provide enough jobs. Once the border had been finally closed, many people were forced to move further away in order to earn a secure living. The "Zonal Border Areas" adjacent to the GDR were at risk of being left out of the general economic improvement. It was for this reason that, as early as 1950, the young federal government had taken measures to anticipate the foreseeable problems of the border areas by introducing "zonal border" subsidies, which applied to a strip of territory about 40 kilometres across bordering the GDR or Czechoslovakia from the Baltic coast southwards. The first subsidy catalogue was drawn up in 1953, including credits from the central government and the states, freight grants and special depreciation concessions. At the end of the decade, a general assistance programme for "priority sectors" in the Zonal Border Area was introduced, and from 1965 various skeleton legislative measures regarding financial assistance for these areas were passed. The Federal Spatial Planning Law laid down priorities for federal aid. Top of the list was assistance for West Berlin, followed by the Zonal Border Area and finally other areas regarded as in need of assistance. The Zonal Border Area accounted for almost 20% of the territory of the Federal Republic plus West Berlin, and 12% of its population. Three "priority sectors" were concerned with bringing the quality of life in the border area up to the level of the rest of the country: infrastructure provision, environmental quality, and employment and income. Federal and state subsidies designed to mitigate the consequences of partition remained an important element in the federal government's German policy right up until re-unification. Between 1980 and 1989 alone, independent of any general economic relief in the area bordering on the GDR and Czechoslovakia, almost two billion deutschmarks was approved for individual projects in the Zonal Border Area. These included support for major cultural projects such as the Bayreuth Festivals, and also support for numerous very small businesses. After West Berlin, Bavaria was the major beneficiary of Zonal Border subsidies.

The roads leading into the restricted zone from the rest of the GDR were now closed with barriers and kept under surveillance. 174 through roads, three motorways, and thousands of public and private paths and tracks were rendered impassable. The extensive waterway network between East and West, except for freight traffic on the Mittelland Canal, was declared unusable in both directions. Almost all of the still extant inter-zonal rail connections were totally blocked by tank traps and similar measures. Traffic between the two parts of Germany was now restricted to six rail and five road crossings.

The 10-metre-broad control strip directly adjacent to the border had been established to give the border guards a clear view, and it was regularly raked so that footprints etc. of "border violators" were visible at

Road block on the main B 84 road, view from Hesse towards Thuringia, in the background the inner-German border with watchtower, c. 1960 (Photo: Point Alpha)

any time. Along the demarcation line, the border police erected a barbed-wire fence about 1.2 to 1.5 metres tall. In the following years a border alarm system was installed, remaining in place until the border itself was abolished. On sections of the border considered to be at special risk, hinterland fences were erected, which at this period were also of barbed wire: they sealed off the 500-metre protective zone. Thus, phased from east to west, the border territory and border installations now consisted of the five-kilometre-broad restricted zone, the 500-metre-broad protective strip, the control strip, which was up to ten metres broad, and the barbed-wire fence. It was easy to see, though many people did not realize it at first, that this unmistakable phasing of the security measures proceeded in an east-west direction, in other words was not, as GDR propaganda would have it, designed to deter the "imperialist class enemy", the "Ultras in Bonn". Rather, the government of the "Workers and Peasants' State" was beginning to imprison its own population. Sections of this population, it must be said, were indifferent to this development, or were even prepared to support the measures with more than just words. From autumn 1952, volunteer police auxiliaries actively helped to secure the border hinterland. By 1955 more than 5,000 of these volunteer auxiliaries were active on an unpaid basis along the border with the Federal Republic.

When the Federal Republic attained virtually complete sovereignty with the Paris Treaties of 1955, joining NATO at the same time, the USSR reacted at once. The GDR was also accorded formal sovereignty in the "Treaty on Relations between the GDR and the USSR" in September 1955, and in January 1956 became a member of the Warsaw Pact. Thus two hostile military alliances confronted each other along the inner-German border from the mid-1950s for the following three and a half decades. Exclusive responsibility for border policing in the GDR was transferred on 1 December 1955 to the German Border Police, while Soviet military personnel were only present as advisers. This did not however extend to controls on the Western Allied forces, which maintained their right of ac-

West Berlin warning sign at the sector boundary on Potsdamer Platz, October 1952 (Photo: Landesarchiv Berlin/Gert Schütz)

Sector boundary sign at the Oberbaum Bridge in Berlin between Kreuzberg (US sector) and Friedrichshain (Soviet sector) (Photo: Landesarchiv Berlin/Karl-Heinz Schubert)

cess to the GDR and to East Berlin, just as Soviet forces had a right of access to the Federal Republic and to West Berlin. In the 1956 "Decree on Easing and Regulation of Measures on the Border between the German Democratic Republic and the German Federal Republic" the term "demarcation line" was replaced by the word "border". The West by contrast stuck to the term "demarcation line" or "zonal border" in order to stress the provisional character of a GDR not legitimized by free and democratic elections. On 11 December 1957 it became a criminal offence in the GDR to attempt to leave the country: the official term was "Republikflucht" – "fleeing the republic".

The "Khrushchev Ultimatum" by the Soviet Union, named after its then leader Nikita Sergeyevitch Khrushchev (1894–1971), imposed a massive strain on the international policy of the two opposing power blocs in respect of Germany and Berlin. On 27 November 1958 the USSR declared the rights of the West-

Border between Zossen district (GDR) and Zehlendorf/Düppel district of Berlin (American sector), railway station, crossing-point, 1960 (Photo: Landesarchiv Berlin/Karl-Heinz Schubert)

ern powers in Berlin to have expired, and demanded for West Berlin the status of a "free, demilitarized city"; failure to comply would result in the Soviet occupation rights in Berlin being transferred to the GDR. The subsequent foreign ministers' conference in Geneva, with the foreign ministers of the two German states present as observers, together with the protest of the Western Allies at the end of the year, meant that nothing came of the ultimatum. On 15 March 1959 the Soviet Union finally recognized the existing rights of the Western occupying powers in Berlin.

In the late 1950s, the GDR leadership extended the strengthening of the inner-German border "friendwards" – to use the jargon of the military. Deep ditches were dug in front of towns and villages near the border to prevent any crossing of the border in vehicles. The first of the up to ten-metre-tall watchtowers were erected, and the first, simple barbed-wire fence was gradually replaced by double fences with concrete

GDR border guards on the watchtower at the inner-German border, 4 May 1959 (Photo: Bundesarchiv Koblenz/ZB Weiss/Bild: 183-63928-0006)

posts. Observation posts, and later, small concrete bunkers, were built, each housing two guards. With the laying of the first mines at about the same time, the inner-German border increasingly became a death-trap. Even so, tens of thousands of people still succeeded in crossing it in the 1950s. For those for whom this was too dangerous, there was still the safe route across the open border to the Western sectors of Berlin. A local train ticket on the Berlin city transport network was still an admission ticket to (hoped for) freedom.

13 AUGUST 1961 TO 1989: THE BERLIN WALL AND REINFORCEMENT OF THE INNER-GERMAN BORDER

In summer 1961, a good ten years after its foundation, the GDR was faced by economic collapse. The massive, and in many cases forcible "collectivization of agriculture" in the "Agricultural Production Co-operatives" or LPGs, the difficult development of the nationalized enterprises known as "People's Own Factories" (German abbreviation: VEB) and the serious restrictions placed on private craft trades was creating serious turbulence for the GDR economy as the 1960s dawned. These forcible measures, combined with worsening supply bottlenecks for the public, political repression, ideologization in almost all spheres of society and of course the enticements of the West German economic miracle all combined to catapult the numbers of those leaving for the West to hitherto unheard-of heights, particularly in 1961. After so many years, many people no longer believed the propaganda put out by the GDR state and party leadership, which sought to present socialism as the more successful system.

From January to August 1961 inclusive, 180,737 inhabitants of the GDR left the country via the Berlin "bolt-hole". It was not only Germans: numerous people from the neighbouring communist states of Poland and Czechoslovakia used Berlin as a springboard for the West. In addition, more than 50,000 East Germans and East Berliners worked in West Berlin, and some 12,000 West Berliners in the East. During 1961 pressure on East Germans working in West Berlin increased considerably. In the summer the GDR au-

GDR pro-paganda poster directed at East Berliners who had a job in the West; it reads "Border-crossers: shame on you!" (design: Leo Haas), 3 August 1961 (Photo: Bundesarchiv Koblenz, 183-85187-0001)

thorities began subjecting them to greatly increased controls, withdrawing their passports and imposing reporting requirements. The Western Allies protested against these restrictions on 3 August. There was an increasing realization in the West that the GDR leadership was preparing a final solution to the problem of refugees and cross-border workers, but no one on the Western side knew what form this solution would take, or when it would happen. In this connexion, the words of GDR head of state and party boss Walter Ulbricht (1893–1973) in answer to a West German reporter's question on 15 June 1961, have become legendary: "No one intends to build a wall."

Between 3 and 5 August 1961, the leaders of the Communist Parties of the Warsaw Pact states met in Moscow. The party leadership of the East German SED was criticized for the country's sluggish economic growth and excessive expenditure on personal consumption. In this connexion, Walter Ulbricht put the main blame on the open border to the Western sectors of Berlin. This argument was finally accepted by the Communist Party of the Soviet Union and the others represented at the conference. Ulbricht was given the go-ahead to seal the border with West Berlin. This represented the foundation stone for all subsequent decisions by the SED leadership and the GDR government. Plans were rapidly made for the final closure of the border in Berlin and thus for the preservation of the GDR. In order to keep the planned measures secret, few were initiated into their existence. The GDR parliament and council of ministers now formally implemented the dictates of the party leadership regarding the solution of the "West Berlin problem". Journeys by GDR citizens to West Berlin were from now on to be subject to approval by the police, and the Interior Ministry was charged with drawing up a new set of border regulations. The parliament and Council of Ministers issued the corresponding decrees. Following a session of the SED politburo on 11 August and the final approval of the measures proposed by the SED, the leading members of the Ministry of State Security now also met, officially for a "celebration". Erich Mielke (1903–2000), who had headed this ministry since 1957, informed the more than 50 high-ranking Stasi officers present that a totally new phase of their work was about to begin, which required the "mobilization of every individual officer". "The current period will show whether we know everything and whether we have roots everywhere. ... No enemy must be allowed to become active, no associations must be allowed to form! ... Those who appear with hostile slogans are to be arrested. ... Enemies are to be dealt with strictly and in the present situation more harshly." By "enemies" of course he meant not the "class enemies" in the West, but those inhabitants of the GDR, who

Crowd of refugees at the Marienfelde Emergency Reception Camp, Berlin, April 1960 (Photo: Landesarchiv Berlin/ Horst Siegmann)

did not agree with the aims of the state, or preferred to leave it. The Stasi was made responsible for securing domestic compliance with the planned border closure, which went ahead under the code names "Rose" and "Ring". On 12 August the SED leadership presented its plans to seal the Berlin border to the commander-in-chief of the Soviet forces in Germany. In the afternoon, Ulbricht signed the orders to implement the measures. Erich Honecker (1912–1994) had already been appointed to head the group charged with seal-

The sealing off of the Soviet sector on 13 August 1961, sector boundary at the Brandenburg Gate, Tiergarten district (Photo: Landesarchiv Berlin/Horst Siegmann)

ing the border; he had already prepared the operation of the border police and general police along with "combat groups of the working class" (Kampfgruppen der Arbeiterklasse). At 10.30 pm Honecker, from 1971 to 1989 SED party boss and GDR head of state, gave the encrypted order for the operation to proceed. At midnight on Saturday/Sunday 12/13 August, the lights on the sector border between East and West Berlin were extinguished. Guards sealed off the border, and the city rail transport to West Berlin was halted completely. The number of road crossing-points from East to West was reduced from more than 80 to, at first, thirteen. The (East) German Border Police pre-

ACHTUNG!
Sie verlassen jetzt
WEST-BERLIN

vented anyone from crossing the sector border: directly
on the border, they, together with units of the People's
Police, formed the first security layer. At the Brandenburg Gate (Brandenburger Tor) and along some
other sections of the border, armed members of the
"combat groups" were also deployed, with heavy sym-
bolism. The second layer, through Berlin and around
West Berlin, was formed by motorized infantry and
tank units, along with intelligence and pioneer units
of the East German National People's Army (Nationale
Volksarmee, NVA). The third security layer, the Soviet occupation forces, were on alert, but remained in
their barracks.

The sealing off of the Soviet sector on 13 August 1961, sector boundary at the Brandenburg Gate, Tiergarten district (Photo: ullstein bild – Georgi)

"The governments of the Warsaw Pact states turn to the parliament and government of the GDR with the proposal to introduce an arrangement on the border to

Berlin, erection of the Wall on 13 August 1961, Oberbaum Bridge, Berlin, Friedrichshain district (Photo: Bundesarchiv Koblenz, Bild: 183854260002)

Berlin, erection of the Wall on 13 August 1961, combat groups at the Brandenburg Gate (Photo: Bundesarchiv Koblenz, Bild: 183-85458-0002)

West Berlin which will reliably put a stop to the subversive activities directed against the countries of the socialist camp and will guarantee reliable surveillance all around the entire territory of West Berlin."

Special bulletin on (East) Berlin Radio at 1.11 am, 13 August 1961 during "Night Melodies".

The Fifth Brigade of the German Border Police stationed on the Berlin Outer Ring Road was given the task, once the border was closed, to dig up the street without delay and to erect a barbed-wire barrier within a week. Controls in West Berlin's hinterland were intensified in order to prevent escapes from the GDR, or protest actions. Even so, by the end of 1961 a further 8,500 people had crossed the barriers between the two German states and around West Berlin, and more than 3,400 GDR citizens were arrested for attempted or planned "flight from the republic". The first sections of wall on the border in Berlin had already gone up by 15 August. Civilian construction workers were also involved in this work, heavily guarded by the Border Police and "combat groups". The first sections of the wall around West Berlin consisted to start with of blocks of stone and simple bricks, and stood about 1.80 metres high, with an original thickness of about 30 cm. The wall was surmounted by barbed wire to prevent people climbing over it. Little by little, there arose one of the most symbolic structures in German history, the Berlin Wall. To accompany the sealing-off of West Berlin, other major steps were taken in the border region. Windows and doors of buildings close to the bor-

Berlin, erection of the Wall, mothers with children at the barbed wire after the first road blocks, August 1961 (Photo: ullstein bild – Hilde)

Berlin, erection of the Wall, 13 August 1961, barbed-wire entanglement at Potsdamer Platz (Photo: ullstein bild Alex Waidmann)

der, such as on Bernauer Strasse, were bricked up or barred, as were station entrances, sewers and other escape routes for GDR citizens.

"On the basis of the decision of the government of the German Democratic Republic taken on 12 August 1961,

the Minister of the Interior issues the following decree with immediate effect:

1. For road traffic for motor and other vehicles and for pedestrians between West Berlin and democratic Berlin, the following crossing points remain open:

Kopenhagener Strasse, Wollankstrasse, Bornholmer Strasse, Brunnenstrasse, Chausseestrasse, Brandenburger Tor, Friedrichstrasse, Heinrich-Heine-Strasse, Oberbaumbrücke, Puschkinallee, Elsenstrasse, Sonnenallee, Rudower Strasse.

2. Citizens of the German Democratic Republic including citizens of the capital of the German Democratic Republic (democratic Berlin) wishing to visit West Berlin require a permit from their local People's Police authority. A separate announcement will be made regarding the issue of such permits.

3. Peaceable citizens of West Berlin may cross to democratic Berlin at the crossing points on production of their West Berlin identity card.

4. Inhabitants of West Germany will be given day permits, as hitherto, to visit the capital of the German De-

Visit by Walter Ulbricht, 1st Secretary of the SED and President of the GDR State Council, to the Berlin Wall, 15 August 1961 (Photo: Bundesarchiv Koblenz, 183-85476-0001)

Boy in front of a road-block with a special edition of the "Berliner Morgenpost";
the headline reads: "East Berlin sealed off" (Photo: ullstein bild – Georgi)

mocratic Republic (democratic Berlin) on production of their personal papers (identity card or passport) at the four issuing offices: Wollankstrasse, Brandenburg Gate, Elsenstrasse, Friedrichstrasse Station.

5. For citizens of other countries, the existing regulations remain in force. For members of the Diplomatic Corps and the Western occupying forces, the present arrangements remain in force.

6. Citizens of the German Democratic Republic who do not work in Berlin are requested not to undertake journeys to Berlin until further notice.

Berlin, 12 August 1961
Maron, Minister of the Interior"

Berlin, the carriageway of Friedrich Ebert Strasse is torn up for the foundations of the Wall, August 1961 (Photo: ullsteinbild – von der Becke)

A 77-year-old woman escapes from her window into West Berlin, as SED officials seek to pull her back, Bernauer Strasse, September 1961 (Photo: ullstein bild – dpa)

The population of Berlin and the two German states were speechless. Even before the fateful night of 13 August was over, numerous people from the East of the city sought to escape via border sections that had not yet been sealed, e.g. across the hitherto largely

Escape from East Berlin out of the window. The pavement in front of the apartment block is in West Berlin. Bernauer Strasse, Berlin, Mitte district (East) and Wedding district (West), 17 August 1961 (Photo: Landesarchiv Berlin/Horst Siegmann)

VOLKSWACHT
ORGAN DER BEZIRKSLEITUNG GERA DER SOZIALISTISCHEN EINHEITSPARTEI DEUTSCHLANDS

Erklärung der Regierungen der Warschauer-Vertrags-Staaten

Wir sichern unsere Grenzen!

Warschauer-Vertrags-Staaten richten Ansuchen an Regierung der DDR
Maßnahmen gegen Wühltätigkeit aus Westberlin getroffen

Leading article prescribed for all GDR newspapers on 14 August 1961, here for the "Volkswacht" in Gera (Repro: Stadtarchiv Gera)

open waterways. On the day of the border closure
there were various protest actions on both sides of the
border. The largest of these, involving more than 3,000
young people, took place on the West Berlin side of
the Brandenburg Gate on the evening of 13 August,
and was broken up by the West Berlin police. The
West Berlin city government had already issued a note
expressing the expectation "that the Western powers
would make an energetic protest to the Soviet government". The city commandants of the Western Al-

*Above: Bernauer Strasse, Berlin, bricking up windows
(Photo: ullstein bild – Gadewoltz)
Right: West Berliners on Bernauer Strasse waving to East
Berlin, 8 September 1961 (Photo: ullstein bild – UPI)
Conversation at the border in Harzer Strasse, Berlin,
Neukölln district, on the boundary with East Berlin, 23
August 1961 (Photo: Landesarchiv Berlin/Horst Siegmann)*

lies ordered the ruling mayor Willy Brandt (1913–1992), however, to protect the border from attacks from West Berlin. The Western Allies were not interested in an escalation of the "Berlin question", as there was a risk of war between the great powers and their respective military alliances. The SED party bosses, who were not sure how the Western powers would react, stationed five motorized infantry regiments in the Berlin hinterland in case of a military counterstrike by the Allies. John F. Kennedy (1917–1963), president of the USA, had however, just one day after the border in Berlin was sealed, let it be known: "A wall is a hell of a lot better than a war." On 19 August he sent his vice-president, the future president Lyndon B. Johnson (1908 –1973), to West Berlin, who reinforced the determination of the USA to stand behind the city. Kennedy himself visited West Berlin on 26 June 1963. At Checkpoint Charlie, the crossing-point on Friedrichstrasse, and at the Brandenburg Gate, curtained off on the GDR side, he viewed the Berlin Wall, and then, in the presence of 300,000 people made a speech outside the Schöneberg Town Hall. His emotional "Ich bin ein Berliner!", spoken in German, is still one of the most-quoted phrases in German history. Guided by the responsible politicians on either side, high-ranking political guests of both German states were shown the GDR border installations above all at the Brandenburg Gate. But while it was granted to state visitors on both sides, it was only in the West that the "mere" people were allowed to inspect the installations. Numerous observation platforms were erected along the Wall, and along the internal German border. "Taking a look at the Wall" soon became a popular tourist attraction especially for visitors to West Berlin.

The reticence of the Western Allies was assessed by the SED and GDR leadership as a political success on their part. The measures to secure the GDR state bor-

President John F. Kennedy goes on a city tour during his visit to Berlin:
viewing the Wall at the sector boundary, Friedrichstrasse, Berlin,
Kreuzberg district, 26 June 1963 (Photo: Landesarchiv Berlin)

der had, according to their propaganda, rescued peace
in Europe, and dealt out the most serious defeat to the
"imperialism of the FRG" since the GDR was formed,
altering the balance of forces in favour of socialism
and thus proving the historical superiority of the ideology: a superiority which had now manifested itself
in locking in its own citizens. Just eleven days after the
Berlin border was sealed, on 24 August, the first
would-be refugee died in a hail of bullets fired by the
GDR Border Police. By 1989, on the Berlin Wall alone,
134 people (information as of 2008) had lost their lives
trying to escape. As already in 1952, there followed a
forced resettlement of those living in the border areas
in the GDR and East Berlin. More than 3,000 people
had to leave their homes by 3 October 1961. At the
same time, buildings and parts of building along the
border were demolished where they impeded the now
increased surveillance. On the inner-German border

too, further buildings and in some cases entire villages were pulled down in the succeeding years as the border installations were strengthened.

The closure of the border in Berlin struck at a pulsating metropolis which had in varying measure just recovered from the effects of the Second World War. Hundreds of thousands of people had crossed the sector borders in both directions every day in order to meet friends and relations, to go shopping, or to go to the cinema, a concert, a museum or the theatre, or simply to have their hair cut. Now everything was divided: families who sometimes lived only on opposite sides of the street, friendships, workmates and lovers. On 23 August 1961, finally, the crossing-points to East Berlin were closed to West Berliners, even though just a few days earlier the East German Interior Minister had promised free access to East Berlin. This removed the last possibility of personal contact except for signals across the boundary and the mail, telephone connections having been cut for a while. Parents were not allowed to visit their children, or grandchildren their grandparents. Nor did the GDR grant entry or exit

GDR propaganda: an "apartment house community" in Bitterfeld hangs up a propaganda notice, 29 August 1961 (Photo: Bundesarchiv Koblenz, Bild: 183-85869-0001)

Building the Berlin Wall, autumn 1961 (Photo: Landesarchiv Berlin)

permits for family celebrations or even for funerals of mothers, fathers or siblings. Only after the Permit Agreement of 17 December 1963 were West Berliners, 28 months after the border closure, once again allowed to visit the Eastern part of the city, albeit for a

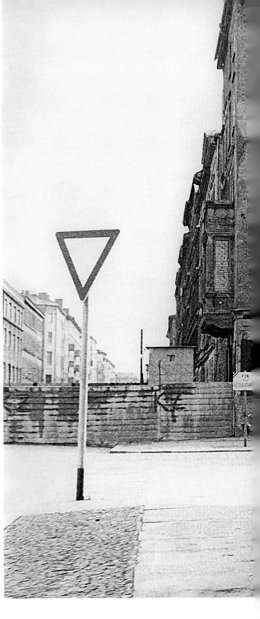

West Berlin, Bernauer Strasse at the end of 1962 with bricked-up windows; the Wall can be seen on the left (Photo: Günter Zint)

restricted period. For the overwhelming majority of the GDR population it was not until the late 1980s that they were able once again to visit the Federal Republic or West Berlin.

In a campaign hitherto unparalleled in the GDR, the border closure of 13 August was followed by a flood of opinions "from the people" asserting their support

for the "securing of the border". Above all the SED regional press and the local organs of the parties in the SED bloc saw a huge wave of propaganda. The fault for the closure of the border, allegedly, had to be borne by "West German warmongers", "people-traders", and "Bonn Ultras" with their influence over misled citizens of the GDR.

"Same standards for all?
'Why should West Berliners be allowed to come across to us, and why can't we cross to West Berlin? I heard that quite often yesterday,' commented colleague Röhricht at the works meeting in the headquarters of Bau-Union Gera. – Any honest person can come to us. There's no trade in people among us, no money-changers, no espionage organizations, no horror cinemas, no gaming hells, warmongering etc. So people can come to us, but we can't go to that Nazi quagmire, the front city of West Berlin. In West Berlin there's a danger of running into disaster. We can't apply the same standards, because we're talking about two fundamentally different systems."

"Volkswacht" newspaper,
organ of the SED party leadership in Gera,
15 August 1961

Forced evacuation of the allotments on Klemkestrasse in East Berlin near the sector boundary between Reinickendorf (West) and Schönholz (East) on 26 September 1961 (Photo: Landesarchiv Berlin/Horst Siegmann)

US tanks at the Checkpoint Charlie crossing-point on Friedrich-strasse, Berlin, Kreuzberg district, 27 October 1961 (Photo: Landesarchiv Berlin/Horst Siegmann)

The propaganda campaign on the part of the SED leadership was implemented in particular in the border areas of Berlin and along the inner-German border in order to adjust the public to the massive sealing-off of the "Workers and Peasants' State". In workplaces and residential areas, many people were pressured to write so-called "solidarity messages" for the "measures" implemented by the GDR leadership. While the huge criticism of the border closure on the part of large sections of the GDR population was not published by the state-controlled GDR media, it was meticulously registered and evaluated by the Stasi, the People's Police and the SED leadership. The rise in the number of trials and other measures against citizens who were not in agreement with the policy of their government was reflected in court statistics. While in the first six months of the year there had been 4,442 political convictions in the GDR, the number of convictions for "political offences" rose in the

Soviet tanks at the sector boundary on Friedrichstrasse, Berlin, Mitte district, 28 October 1961 (Photo: Landesarchiv Berlin/Karl-Heinz Schubert)

second half of 1961 to 18,297. With the closing of the border and the construction of the Wall around West Berlin, the "Berlin problem" for the GDR, the USSR, and also for the Western powers did however seem to have eased to some extent, albeit at the expense of the people in both halves of Germany and in Berlin.

A confrontation at Checkpoint Charlie in the heart of Berlin in October 1961 did though give some idea of the sensitivity of the situation between the two great powers. On the evening of 22 October a member of the US mission in West Berlin, together with his wife, was required by a GDR border guard to produce his identity papers when crossing the border. The American refused, as such a check would have infringed Allied rights. Later, accompanied by an armed escort, he proceeded to cross the border without identifica-

tion, as did other Americans in the next few days. After British diplomats had shown their papers to GDR border police without any argument on 25 October, General Clay, that very same day, ordered American tanks to draw up along the Western section of Friedrichstrasse. The next day Soviet tanks drew up on the Eastern section of the street. For the first time since the start of the "Cold War", the tanks of the two big powers and former allies were facing each other at a distance of some 200 metres. On 28 October both sides withdrew. The show of strength came to a rapid end. An escalation of the conflict was not in the interest of either superpower. Representatives of the Western Allies continued to enjoy uncontrolled access to East Berlin. From 19 August 1961, as the Berlin Wall began to take shape, it became the venue of a curious propaganda war. On the initiative of the member of the West Berlin administration responsible for internal affairs, and financed by the West Berlin government, the so-called "Studio am Stacheldraht" ("Studio at the Barbed Wire) or SAS started "broadcasting". The idea was to use huge loudspeakers, which were later attached to movable cranes, to relay the slogan "Germans don't shoot at Germans", and thus to influence the actions of East German border guards in particular. Much to the annoyance of the GDR party and state leadership, current news programmes were also relayed, and loud enough to be heard well into East Berlin territory. In return, the East German National People's Army set up loudspeakers to address West Berlin. It was not until 1965 that this "loudspeaker war" ended. Alongside attempts to influence the other side acoustically, visual propaganda also soon appeared. Thus the Springer skyscraper on Potsdamer Platz in the middle of Berlin and not far from the Wall displayed huge modern illuminated signs with political news for East Berliners and their visitors. From the Western side, often on private initiative, for example that of the newly formed "Arbeitsgemeinschaft 13. August" ("13 August Working-Group"), border soldiers in the East were exhorted not to use their weapons. GDR propaganda was more robust: "Those who attack us will be annihilated," was one such martial slogan on the placards erected on the eastern side.

Only 14 days after the almost hermetic sealing of the border, the party and state bosses in the GDR embarked on their biggest campaign to date to recruit volunteers for service in the National People's Army. Instrumentalized for this elaborately staged enterprise was the Free German Youth (Freie Deutsche Jugend, FDJ), the GDR's state youth organization, in effect the youth wing of the SED. The "call to arms of the FDJ", with its slogan "The fatherland calls – protect the socialist republic", in the style of "Your Country Needs

Sector boundary, Potsdamer Platz. In the background, the ruin of the "Haus Vaterland" complex, Berlin, Mitte district (East) seen from West Berlin, 1962 (Photo: Landesarchiv Berlin)

Loudspeaker vans operated by the West Berlin city administration at the Wall in Stresemannstrasse/Dessauer Strasse, Berlin, Kreuzberg district, 28 July 1962 (Photo: Landesarchiv Berlin)

You", resembled a mobilization campaign in schools, universities, factories and other institutions, and was hyped in the GDR as a "national event". According to the GDR, more than 170,000 young men volunteered for military service as a result. The National People's Army and the German Border Police were at this time recruited from volunteers, but the number coming forward was declining. The recruitment campaign, similar to that which followed the events of 17 June 1953 in the early years of the GDR, and with similar pressure from above, represented an attempt by the GDR leadership to psychologically prepare their now captive "working population" for the introduction of compulsory military service and thus also for the integration of the Border Police into the National People's

Berlin sector boundary, beyond is Mitte district in East Berlin, intersection of Zimmerstrasse and Lindenstrasse.
Left: notice in four languages to the start of the American sector
Right: Berlin Wall, Kreuzberg district, 5 January 1965 (Photo: Landesarchiv Berlin/Ludwig Ehlers)

Two GDR border guards on patrol, in the background Hanstein Castle in the Eichsfeld. This important fortress is close to where the state borders of Lower Saxony, Hesse and Thuringia meet. One of its towers was used as a watchtower by the GDR border guards. February 1965 (Photo: Bundesarchiv Koblenz/ZB Kohls)

Army. Conscription was finally introduced in the GDR by a law of 24 January 1962.

The closure of the Berlin sector border led to increased refugee pressure along the inner-German border, which, while heavily guarded since 1952, was not yet technically perfect. As early as 14 September 1961, therefore, the commander-in-chief of the Soviet forces in Germany recommended the GDR government to strengthen the "Western border of the state". In connexion with the final closure of the border, the German Border Police was integrated into the National

People's Army as the "Border Command" on 15 September 1961, and thus placed under the control of the GDR Defence Ministry. In November 1961 the Coastal Border Brigade started, on its own account, to secure the GDR's maritime border. In August 1962, with the formation of a "City Command for the Capital of the GDR", the Berlin units of the Border Police were also placed under the control of the Defence Ministry. Thus all the units responsible for defending the border finally came under the control of one ministry. New weapons, an improvement in specialized training, the rigorous strengthening of the border installations and finally the transition from the voluntary principle to the selection of specially vetted conscripts made it possible to achieve a high degree of perfection on the "Western border of the state".

At a session held in November 1961, the GDR National Defence Council, whose secretary at this time was Erich Honecker, took the decision to massively reinforce the state border by November 1962 in order to heavily reduce the number of those fleeing the republic. It was apparent to the GDR leadership that they could not build a "Berlin Wall" along the whole 1400-kilometre length of the inner-German border. In January 1963 army general Karl Heinz Hoffmann (1910–1985), GDR Minister of National Defence, announced that most of the plans had been implemented. By this time, 885 kilometres of double barbed-wire fencing had been completed. Over 447 kilometres, various types of mine were laid. By 1983, ultimately more than a million landmines had been laid, and numerous people had been killed or maimed. 490 kilometres of additional roadblocks and 96 wooden watch-towers were built, and along 425 kilometres, the border guards cut a swathe up to 200 metres broad through the forest in order to provide an unimpeded view, and allowing them to take unimpeded aim.

Access to a factory in the border area of East Berlin, Treptow district, 22 June 1963 (Photo: Bundesarchiv Koblenz, 183-B0622-0007-001)

These border installations were extended and "improved" on an ongoing basis.

Already on 20 September 1961 Erich Honecker had demanded "the taking of measures against traitors and border violators which would allow criminals to be trapped in the 100-metre restricted zone." In consequence, the GDR Defence Minister issued Order No. 76/61 in October of that year, which contained the "Directives for Border Command of the National People's Army on the use of firearms". The existing directives on firearm use (service regulation 10/4) were revised and extended in various points. The "top secret" memorandum of the GDR government thus formed the basis for the shoot-to-kill policy which was to be implemented especially by the young conscripts at the bottom of the command chain, many of whom had to wrestle severely with their conscience.

Passierschein I 1076217

zum vorübergehenden Aufenthalt im Schutzstreifen

Herr / Frau / Fräulein ████████████

(Name)
Hans

(Vorname)
am 20.10.1989

ist berechtigt, sich aus ~~dienstlichen~~ / **privaten** Gründen in der Zeit vom .... bis ....

in **Babelsberg Krs.-**

(Ort und Kreis)
Potsdam-Stadt .... aufzuhalten.

Der Passierschein ist **nur gültig** in Verbindung mit dem Personalausweis Nr. **E 0002155**

Mitgeführtes Kraftfahrzeug (pol. Kennz.) **----**

Potsdam 1 0. Okt. 1989

Hinweise auf der Rückseite beachten! ...., den .... 19....

(Unterschrift)

PM 107 (87/11) Ag 106/82/83/84/85

Permit for the "protective strip" in the border zone, Potsdam-Babelsberg, 20 October 1989 (Photo: Führ)

"... guards and patrols of the border units of the National People's Army based on the western border of the state and on the coast will use firearms in the following cases: ...

to arrest persons who do not comply with the instructions of the border guards in that they do not stand still on being given the order: "Halt! Stop where you are! Border guard!" or after a warning shot has been fired, but obviously attempt to violate the state border of the German Democratic Republic, and no other possibility of arrest exists;

to arrest persons who use vehicles of whatever kind in an obvious attempt to violate the state border, having not complied with a stop signal given by the border guard in the prescribed manner or do not react to a warning shot, or, after they have broken through, removed or driven around a road block, there is no other possibility of arresting the persons concerned.

2. Firearms used against the border violator will only be fired in the direction of the territory of the GDR or parallel to the state border.

Barbed wire is replaced by concrete tubes on the Wall in Lindentrasse in the Mitte district of Berlin, 1966 (Photo: ullstein bild – Wieczorek)

3. Firearms will not be used
against members of foreign armies and military liaison missions, against members of diplomatic missions, against children ..."

Order of the Minister of National Defence,
No. 76/61, October 1961

On 21 May 1963 a decision was taken to set up a special border zone around West Berlin. The border zone at the Berlin Wall was only to be entered with a special permit. It was between 40 metres and 2.5 kilometres across, calculated from the hinterland fence or the hinterland wall that was subsequently built. The latter installations formed the visible border on the Eastern side. As already since 1952 along the inner-German border, the 120,000 or so East Berliners who lived and worked in this zone were now under constant surveillance. Any relation or tradesperson who wished to access the border zone to visit or to work was required to obtain a permit for the zone. Dwelling close to the Wall was a major strain for most of those involved. The brightly lit border strip with its lethal defences, guarded and watched around the clock, seriously impaired the quality of life.

By August 1964 there was 15 kilometres of Wall around West Berlin, and 130 kilometres of barbed-wire entanglement, along with 165 watchtowers, mostly of wood. The border strip was not yet illuminated everywhere, nor was there yet an uninterrupted patrol track. The cost of the measures in Berlin had already mounted up to 56.5 million East German marks by this time. Even so, numerous people still succeeded in overcoming the security measures and escaping to the West. It was also still easy for GDR border guards to make cross-border contact. After massive criticism on the part of the SED leadership, a detailed plan was put forward by the border guards to strengthen the border around West Berlin. The plan provided among other things for an extension and renewal of the Wall, a strengthening of the border fence, humps and other obstacles for vehicles, an uninterrupted patrol track, uninterrupted illumination of the border, the erection of 150 new watchtowers, this time of concrete, new guard-houses, two-man bunkers, 130 kilometres of alarmed fence, and 271 toilets – all by 1970. The cost was estimated at almost 37 million East German marks. This was equivalent to some 224,000 marks per kilometre for the border around West Berlin. Because of the narrow border strip on the Berlin border, and for fear of international protests, mines and spring-guns were not planned.

This plan went into effect from 1966. The focus was on the extension of the Wall, which was now constructed of prefabricated concrete slabs with horizontal joins, with a smooth concrete tube on top. From now on this standardized and visually cold system was the face the border around West Berlin showed to the

Blowing up buildings on Bernauer Strasse on 29 December 1965 to make room for the Berlin Wall. The Church of Reconciliation in the background survived until 1985. (Photo: ullstein bild)

world. In the 1970s, the border strip in front of the Berlin Wall was broadened in order to arrest refugees as far as possible from the final great obstacle. From 1974, the hinterland wall and the alarmed border fence were built up. For people from the East, the country came not just visibly to an end here. Any further step over the hinterland wall or the hinterland fence towards the Berlin Wall itself was potentially lethal. From the Western side, by contrast, it was perfectly simple to approach right up to the Wall, which, while entirely on GDR territory, was accessible to anyone in the West. Allotment owners in West Berlin used it to grow plants against, children used it for games. From the mid-1970s, the West side of the Wall became a favourite surface for messages and art of all

Berlin, Potsdamer Platz, view from West to East, c. 1965 (Photo: Günter Zint)

kinds. GDR border guards often pulled down illegal
structures put up by West Berliners on the "rear" of
the Wall. But the Berlin Wall remained until its fall

doubtless the biggest informal-art surface in the world. Initial complaints by the GDR leadership to the West Berlin city authorities were ignored, and overpainting of sections of Wall by GDR border guards re-

GDR border troops working on the Berlin Wall, Harzer Strasse, Berlin, Neukölln district, April 1980, view from West to East (Photo: Wolfgang Kramer)

GDR border troops working on the Berlin Wall, Waldemarstrasse, view from West Berlin (Kreuzberg district) eastwards, March 1984 (Photo: Wolfgang Kramer)90

Above and below: view of the Berlin Wall looking east from St. Thomas' church, Berlin, Kreuzberg district, August 1985 (Photo: Wolfgang Kramer)

mained equally ineffectual. After 1966 pioneer units of the border guard constructed anti-vehicle ditches on the inner-German border and around West Berlin. These ditches were dug in front of the two rows of barbed-wire entanglement, and were about three metres across and 1.50 metres deep, while the side nearest the West was lined with oblique concrete slabs in order to prevent vehicles breaking through from East to West. From 1967/68 the barbed-wire fence was gradually replaced by a barred fence of expanded-metal plates (border fence I). The existing unmetalled patrol tracks were covered in concrete slabs the same year, in order to guarantee the border guards' mobility. The patrol track was used by the border guards for foot or motorized patrols. Alongside it was an "evidence-securing strip" – the K 6 control strip with a breadth of about six metres, which was examined daily for signs of "border violation".

Already in the test phase since the start of 1967, and finalized in August of that year, 2,622 border pillars, 13 border buoys and 9,079 border stones were installed along the inner-German border. In this way the GDR sought to manifest its view of the course of the "state border". The border pillars, painted with diagonal black, red and gold stripes, were positioned on the "advance sovereign territory" of the GDR, a few metres in front of the first installations (mostly a wire-mesh fence or the Wall) and behind the actual line of the border. A GDR emblem, originally of plastic, was placed on the side facing the Federal Republic. Between 1973 and 1978 the existing Joint Border Commission of the Federal Republic and the GDR examined the border markers, with the result that by common agreement some individual border stones were shifted. From 1968 difficult-to-monitor sections both along the inner-German border and the Berlin Wall were additionally secured by dogs attached to leads allowing them to run freely: their purpose was primarily to report the pres-

Border installations in the divided village of Mödlareuth; on the right GDR border guards can be seen securing the border, while on the left West German customs officers look on. The rope marks the border, 20 October 1964 (Photo: ullstein bild – AP)

The Wall in the divided village of Mödlareuth; view eastwards from the Bavarian part, July 1969 (Photo: ullstein bild – Lehnartz)

ence of would-be refugees. In 1969 the first round watchtowers of prefabricated concrete components were erected, replacing the existing wooden towers. At various particularly endangered sections of the border, e.g. the crossing-points, in populated towns along the inner-German border and above all along the Berlin Wall, illumination facilities were installed. The modern halogen lamps were mostly secured to thin, curved masts. As an important means of "border security", the National People's Army border units deployed signal equipment from the mid 1960s. These devices, equipped with flare cartridges of different colours, were triggered by a string over the ground, and a border guard, with the help of a signal table, could then pinpoint the site of the attempted border violation. In 1967 pioneer units of the border guard started erecting Border Fence I, which was gradually to replace the double barbed-wire fence. While all the

A spring-gun installation is dismantled at the wire-mesh fence on the GDR side; border between Thuringia and Hesse, 1970s (Photo: Point Alpha)

GDR watchtower between Rasdorf and Setzelbach (Thuringia); in the foreground, a GDR border marker, after 1970 (Photo: Point Alpha)

technical measures taken by the GDR to secure the border, along with improved training for the guards, succeeded in greatly reducing the number of "border violations" and desertions, they could not alter the fact that the Wall was the international "hallmark" of the East German state.

Among the numerous curiosities of the inner-German border were the towns and villages which, like Berlin, were divided into Eastern and Western halves by the post-war developments. The most striking example was doubtless the village of Mödlareuth on the border between Thuringia and Bavaria. The village had already been divided in previous centuries as a result of territorial disputes between feudal overlords. One part finally fell to the kingdom of Bavaria, while the other remained with the Thuringian principality of Reuss (Junior Line). There was nothing particularly serious about that, as borders in German history, while they meant there were legal differences between the places thus divided, did not in any way restrict freedom of movement. After the end of the Second World War, one half of the village found itself in the American zone, while the other was in the Soviet zone. At this stage, the village children still went to one village school, and their parents still met in one village pub. When the two German states were formed in 1949, the two halves found themselves belonging to systems moving in opposite political, economic and military directions. The village stream could now only be crossed with a permit. From 1952, the new GDR border decree imposed the restricted zone, protective strip and control strip on the inhabitants, and finally a two-metre wooden fence surmounted by steel spikes. In 1966, on the pattern of the Berlin Wall, a concrete wall 3.30 metres high and 700 metres long was erected through the village. Lit up at night, and equipped with corresponding additional security technology, and under constant surveillance from a watchtower, the remote village became a particularly well-guarded section of the inner-German border. The place at the end of two worlds became known worldwide as "Little Berlin", and symbolized the idiocy of the inner-German border to an exceptional degree. Some 25 kilometres of concrete walling was also used along other difficult-to-monitor sections of the inner-German border.

On the basis of a decision of the GDR National Defence Council of 23 October 1969 the border units of the army were completely restructured in the spring of 1971. The border brigades, or in the case of Berlin the border security forces of the Berlin city command, were replaced by the Border Commands North (based in Stendal), Central (based in Karlshorst, Berlin) and South (based in Erfurt), all subordinate to "Border Command" with its headquarters in Pätz near Berlin. Each of the three border commands consisted of six regiments. The Border Command Central exceptionally included artillery units, the only border unit to be

Corporal of the 7th Border Brigade (Magdeburg) of the NVA, 1970. The typical distinctive feature of GDR border guards was a photo in front of the flag (emblem: "for the protection of worker and peasant power"). (Photo: Führ)

armed thus, with Russian-made rocket-launchers, flame-throwers, cannon, howitzers and grenade-launchers. In this case, the plan was, in an "emergency", that West Berlin should be attacked, or as the case might be, that these special units should be the first line of defence should the Allies launch an attack from West Berlin. The technical equipment of the border troops also included helicopters and power-boats for the inland waterways. The border units on the coast continued to be under the command of the "People's Navy". One border regiment was stationed on the border with Poland, and another on the Czech border. All in all, the strength of the GDR border troops in the 1970s was more than 50,000 men.

Since the introduction of conscription in the GDR in 1962, recruits had been automatically conscripted into service with the border units. They had to undergo intense vetting by the security organs of the GDR, such as the People's Police and the Stasi. The young conscripts had to fit into a pattern that as far as possible excluded the possibility of desertion while serving on the border, and guaranteed that they would, if necessary, shoot at refugees attempting to cross the border. Among other things, their family contacts were checked, as were any contacts with Westerners, their future career aims, and their partners. If a conscript was selected for service on the border, he would often not hear about it until the day he joined up. After basic military training lasting four weeks, the young soldiers were given specialized training in the training units of the border regiments. This training was tailored to their future service on the border. Only in the second six-month period of the eighteen-month term of military service were the border soldiers actually deployed on the inner-German border and in Berlin, on the front line, so to speak. In spite of somewhat better living conditions and higher pay – they received a "border bonus" – service on the border was not particularly popular. After all, they would be stationed in mostly remote locations, with little time off and not much leave, and above all the duty in shifts was stressful both physically and psychologically. And in spite of official propaganda to the contrary, and undoubted positive contacts with the inhabitants of the border region, it was nevertheless true that especially in the Greater Berlin and Potsdam area, border troops were looked down on. The accusation levelled at many conscripts who had the bad luck to have to serve on the inner-German border, namely that of being a "Mauerschütze" – literally "Wall marksman", i.e. a border guard who would shoot to kill – was a heavy burden. The NCOs on fixed-term contracts, along with the professional soldiers selected for border duty, received their six-month NCO training at the NCO schools in Glöwe or Potsdam, and from 1973 in Perleberg. On 25 February 1971, what had hitherto been a training

"On their patrol the border guards often visit the lumberjacks of the Type III LPG [collective farm] 'Klement Gottwald' in Bornhagen, who worked in the immediate vicinity of the state border. The lumberjacks often tip off the border-guards about strangers and share their observations.", caption by GDR photo agency Zentralbild (ZB) to demonstrate the bonds between the border guards and the inhabitants of the region, 18 February 1965 (Photo: Bundesarchiv Koblenz/ZB Kohls)

school for border troop officers in Plauen (transferred to Suhl in 1983) was raised to the status of a military academy, named after Rosa Luxemburg. Its newly defined profile was tailored to producing company-level officers for service on the border.

Finally, on 1 April 1974, in the run-up to the Vienna disarmament conference staged under the auspices of the Conference on Security and Co-operation in Europe (CSCE), the border units were taken out of National People's Army command, but continued as "border troops of the German Democratic Republic" to be

Inner-German border with border installations, Thuringia/Hesse, early 1980s. Patrol track, anti-vehicle ditch, and border fence I of expanded metal (Photo: Point Alpha)

under the control of the Ministry of Defence, a ploy on the part of the GDR leadership to avoid having them officially counted for the purposes of the international disarmament talks. One visible result of the change was the green armband on the left arm of their uniforms, with the inscription "Border Troops of the GDR".

In spite of the gradually palpable détente in the international political climate, and the increasing contacts between official representatives of the two German states, the GDR leadership held firm to the costly maintenance and strengthening of the border installations right up until the late 1980s. In 1970 the SM 70 splinter mines were first installed, popularly known as "Selbstschussanlagen" or "self-shooting devices", in other words a form of spring-gun. These represented a particularly treacherous weapon deployed to prevent citizens of the GDR from "fleeing the republic". Triggered by a piece of tensed wire, the SM 70 scattered up to 80 sharp-edged metal splinters over an area with a radius of 120 metres, and at short range they were lethal. This form of border defence was, while the com-

Pioneer unit of the GDR border guards searching for mines between wire-mesh fences on the border between Hesse and Thuringia, c. 1985 (Photo: Point Alpha)

munist German state was seeking international diplomatic recognition, for a long time hushed up and indeed denied by the GDR leadership. It was only through border guards who had deserted, and through wounded refugees who had succeeded in making it to West German territory, that the existence of the splinter mines became known in the West. The technically improved version of the "self-shooting devices", deployed from 1976, fired up to 20 steel bullets and was less vulnerable to theft and false alarms, for example by wildlife. In mid 1983 there were some 60,000 of these splinter mines along about 450 kilometres of the inner-German border. It took the ten-figure credits organized by the West German politician Franz-Josef Strauss to persuade the GDR leadership to dismantle all the landmines and "self-shooting devices" from the early 1980s on. This process was completed by 1985. However, even after the border itself was dismantled in 1989/90, some of these mines left in the ground still had to be cleared and defused. Very efficient was the border alarm fence, known by its German abbreviation GSZ 70, which came into use from 1973, and was equipped with both optical and acoustic alarm signals. As a "hinterland fence", the GSZ 70 sealed off the restricted zone along the whole length of the inner-German border. The basic type consisted of an expanded-metal plate, above which a number of strands of barbed wire were stretched. On top of these was an oblique set of four more strands of barbed wire, pointing in the direction of the GDR at an angle of about 45°. If at least two wires touched, or just one was cut, an alarm was set off in one of the border-guard command posts. The numbering of the individual sections allowed the "border violation" (i.e. escape attempt) to be localized with the help of the signals. In the 1980s, the GSZ was replaced by a modernized version, which was virtually impossible to climb over without major technical assistance. The prevention of "border violations" already at the first hinterland fence along the inner-German border was very convenient for the GDR leadership, as they were removed from the international limelight, and unpleasant questions did not have to be answered so frequently. Spectacular arrests and chases involving would-be refugees no longer took place beneath the eyes of Western observers, but rather some way behind the border.

The final obstacle remained the Border Fence I, which extended the whole length of the inner-German border, and was placed just a little inside the boundary of GDR territory. It was on average 3.20 metres high and consisted from the 1980s of concrete posts to each of which three overlapping galvanized extended-metal plates were attached. The sharp-edged grid structure of the plates with their two-centimetre wide lozenge-shaped perforations offered no hand or footholds, and thus had a similar effect to the concrete wall around West Berlin. The gates in the border fence were secured mechanically or electrically. Their purpose was

Watchtower in the border region at the Friedrich Ludwig Jahn Sports Park, East Berlin, Prenzlauer Berg district, 20 July 1973 (Photo: Landesarchiv Berlin)

to provide access for border guards to the strip of GDR territory on the western side of the fence. In a few cases, GDR farmers were permitted to pursue agriculture on this strip between the fence and the actual border, it goes without saying under strict surveillance.

"The National People's Army, the Border Troops of the GDR, the Ministry of State Security, the German People's Police and the other organs of the Ministry of the Interior, the Combat Groups of the Working Class and the members of the Civil Defence are uprightly fulfilling their class responsibility of protecting the socialist order and the peaceful lives of the citizens against all enemies. It remains their task to guarantee the sovereignty, the territorial integrity, the inviolability of the borders and the security of the GDR."

Erich Honecker, Chairman of the State Council of the GDR and General Secretary of the SED, at the 11th SED Party Congress, 1985

The SED and state leadership faced particular challenges when international events were due to take place in East Berlin, or when state or official visits classed as important were due in the GDR or also in the Federal Republic. For these periods, it was considered important to avoid unpleasant incidents such as shooting at would-be refugees on the border. The suspension of the order to shoot was thus given explicitly both by telephone and in writing by the GDR leadership. One of the really major international events was the holding of the "10th World Youth and Student Games" in East Berlin in 1973. More than ten years after the building of the Wall, the GDR attempted to present itself at this meeting of young people from all over the world as a modern and cosmopolitan state. While the young people did not confine themselves to attendance at the major events, and visited the border hinterland until late in the night, a huge presence of Stasi, police, and above all GDR border guards was in a state of heightened alert. For the Border Command Central in Berlin all leave had been cancelled even before the Games began, and the border hinterland all round West Berlin was virtually hermetically sealed off, in order to avoid any border incident no matter how trivial.

In return, members of the border units received better food and in addition limited quantities of alcohol, which was otherwise not available to lower ranks in their barracks. Similar trouble was given to securing the inner-German border and the Berlin Wall when the president of the Soviet Union, Leonid Breschnev (1907–1982), visited Bonn in 1981. In the 1980s too this process was continued, for example on the occasion of Berlin's 750th anniversary in 1987. With the dismantling of the mines on the inner-German border and as a result of internal political developments in the GDR, pressure on the inner-German border and the Berlin Wall increased. As early as 1983, the political and military leadership of the GDR had drawn up detailed plans to adapt the border system to the changed conditions, and to prevent the predictable rise in "border violations". Internationally "negative" actions, such as using firearms to prevent escapes, were to be reduced even further. In 1989 a major restructuring of the GDR Border Troops took place. The three border commands formed in 1971 were abolished and border district commands set up in their place. Thus the structure of the border troops belatedly adapted itself to the political structure in the GDR. A "visually clean" hi-tech border with a "greened" hinterland fence and expensive, highly sensitive electronic surveillance equipment was planned to be in place by 2000 – a plan that was overtaken by events.

OVER HERE AND OVER THERE: TRAVEL AND CONTACTS IN DIVIDED GERMANY

After the end of the Second World War, the Allies had imposed a general travel ban. Long-distance journeys, in particular between the individual occupation zones, generally required a permit. From 1945, such permits were issued by the occupation authorities in exceptional cases. On 29 October 1945, inter-zonal passes were introduced. The British Zone abandoned this regulation as early as 1 November 1948, but within the newly constituted Federal Republic it remained in force for a further year. For travel between the Federal Republic and the GDR, inter-zonal passes were required until 16 November 1953 for West-East travel, and for a further week for travel in the other direction.

After the war, private individuals were forbidden to move goods between the Soviet zone and the Western zones. But the general shortage of goods, as well as inter-zonal private trade, led by the early 1950s to lively exchange in both directions across the zonal border. Although it was already dangerous to life and limb, hundreds of thousands of people crossed the demarcation line in the immediate post-war period. The Soviet guards and the newly formed border police in the Soviet zone and then the GDR were inconsistent in the rigour with which they dealt with illegal border crossings, and from time to time co-operated with authorities on West German territory.

As a result of the GDR customs law passed on 1 May 1950, control points were set up on roads and railways around Berlin to enforce compliance, as also on the Western border of the GDR. Even before the control points were reached, guards belonging to the

Staff of the GDR Office of Customs and Goods Transfer Control at the East German border control point Marienborn (Magdeburg region), 28 July 1954 (Photo: Bundesarchiv Koblenz/ZB Junge)

transport police checked suspicious persons travelling towards Berlin. Those who could not provide sufficient justification for their journey to Berlin or were carrying scarce goods from the GDR were interrogated, sometimes arrested and at the very least deported. The goods were confiscated. In order to prevent "sabotage and disruption by illegal trade and currency smuggling", on 1 September 1951 the GDR set up a "customs and goods-movement office"; known from 1962 as GDR Customs, the office took over some of the functions of the German Border Police, as it then was (see above).

From 13 August 1961 and into the 1970s, travel from the GDR to West Germany and West Berlin was only possible for a highly restricted section of the population. The largest group consisted of pensioners (women over 60, men over 65) and invalids, who were granted a four-week stay in the West per year. This possibility started in November 1964. It was also relatively easy for these groups to move permanently from the GDR to West Germany or West Berlin. The freezing of travel across the inner-German borders after the building of the Wall in 1961 drove the GDR into increasing isolation. For scientists, scholars, and business travellers, permits were subject to the strict criteria applied by the party and state leadership, and were as a result not easily obtained. Travel was only permitted to a highly restricted circle known popularly as "travel cadres". The privilege of belonging to the "travel cadres" was much sought-after. The SED and the Stasi saw to it that only "loyal" citizens were allowed to travel to the West, including to West Germany and West Berlin. The selection procedure focused on political reliability in the sense of the SED, and security questions, especially that regarding the possibility of "fleeing the republic". Having no relations in "the West", and of course no private contacts, was particularly useful. Reports by "unofficial employees" of the Stasi (i.e. informers) contributed to the preliminary vetting. The right of veto and the further surveillance of those with a permit to travel

The Allied Check Point at Helmstedt on the West German (Lower Saxony) side of the border, 10 June 1967 (Photo: Bundesarchiv Koblenz/ZB Link)

Much sought after and mostly only for GDR pensioners: a visa for a journey from East to West, 1969 (Photo: Führ)

abroad were, after all, among the important fields of Stasi activity. In spite of all the rumours circulating at the time and since, however, only a very small proportion of those allowed to travel on economic, cultural, sporting, church or media business were themselves Stasi informers. Even so, the "travel cadres" system created a network of dependencies and loyalties and ultimately served the leadership as a form of control. The restriction of travel imposed by the leadership led to a considerable loss of information above all in the scientific field, which could only in part be compensated for by other sources. Scientific exchange programmes between the GDR and western European states, the USA and not least West Germany were fairly thin on the ground in the 1970s and 80s. For most East Germans, though, travel to foreign countries in the West or to West Germany remained a distant dream, and there was certainly no legal right. This unfulfillable dream and the fantasies of an inaccessible world were to profoundly influence the thinking of large sections of the GDR population.

For West Germans, foreigners, members of the Western occupation forces and diplomats and journalists accredited to East Berlin, the inner-German border and the Wall were not insuperable barriers. West Berliners, by contrast, had more problems after the Wall was built. The special status of West Berlin after the end of the Second World War created a series of problems which were maximally exploited by the GDR leadership. From 23 August 1961 to the end of 1963, West Berliners were forbidden to enter East Berlin or the GDR, except to use the transit routes to West Germany. After lengthy disputes, the GDR government finally issued permits for West Berliners to visit East Berlin at Christmas 1963. The first Permit Agreement with West Berlin involved a decidedly

Permit Agreement, in force from 19 December 1963 – 5 January 1964. East Berlin postal workers bring permits to West Berlin. Invalidenstrasse crossing-point, Berlin, Tiergarten district, December 1963 (Photo: Landesarchiv Berlin)

Throng at the permit-issuing centre in the Schiller School, Schiller-strasse 125, Berlin, Charlottenburg district, 19 December 1963 (Photo: Landesarchiv Berlin/Gert Schütz)

complex issuing procedure. GDR postal employees were despatched to West Berlin to receive applications, but these were actually processed in East Berlin, before the permits were handed out in twelve West Berlin schools and gymnasiums, outside which queues formed in the freezing cold and snow. People waited for up to twelve hours to obtain these much-sought-after documents. After two years, West Berliners could finally embrace their friends and relations in East Berlin once more. In specially approved cases, they could also drive there: Western cars had become an unaccustomed sight on East Berlin streets since the building of the Wall. On Friedrichstrasse and on the Oberbaum bridge – two of the five existing crossing points in Berlin – the GDR authorities had set up numerous temporary processing huts. The opportunity for visits was limited to the period from 19 December 1963 to 5 January 1964. In these two weeks, 1,242,800 permits for day-visits to East Berlin were issued. The permits were valid from 6 am to midnight, and visitors were required to change at least 10 deutschmarks into East German marks at a rate of one-to-one. By Whitsun 1966, there had been three further Permit Agreements for West Berliners to visit East Berlin. After that, West Berliners again had to wait years for another opportunity to visit East Berlin and the GDR. It was not until 29 March 1972 that the GDR government relaxed the regulations.

Negotiations by the four victorious Allies of the Second World War, started in 1970, finally resulted in the Four-Power Agreement on Berlin of 3 September 1971. It led to a huge improvement in relations between the two German states, and also greatly improved the situation of West Berlin. In parallel with the four-power negotiations, at the end of 1970 the two German states started their own bilateral talks on traffic issues, a transit agreement and a basic treaty. The leaders of these negotiations were the state secretaries (junior ministers) Egon Bahr (West) and Michael Kohl (East). These talks resulted in the first legal framework in the GDR for an improvement in travel between the two German states.

The "Treaty between the German Democratic Republic and the government of the Federal Republic of Germany on the Transit of Civilians and Goods between the Federal Republic of Germany and Berlin (West)" became the foundation for transit traffic across GDR territory until the fall of the Wall. This traffic treaty was then followed by the signing of the "Basic Treaty" between the FRG and GDR on 21 December 1972. This latter treaty recognized the four-power responsibility for both states, the inviolability of the borders, the limitation of the exercise of sovereignty by each state to its respective territory, the exchange of "permanent representatives", the retention of "inner-German trade" on special terms, which favoured the East in particular, and a declaration by

Permit Agreement, West Berliners being subjected to checks at the Chausseestrasse crossing-point, 4 January 1964 (Photo: Bundesarchiv Koblenz, 183-C0104-0009-001)

each state that it would not object to UN membership on the part of the other. The Basic Treaty was followed up by a treaty on "local border traffic", under which inhabitants of districts close to the border on either side obtained the possibility of day-visits to the other side. For this purpose, four new crossing-points were set up. East German towns and villages which lay within the GDR restricted zones were excluded from the scheme. Before entering East Germany for the first time, West Germans had to apply for a multiple permit from the GDR passport authorities. This document was as a rule issued after four to six weeks, and was valid for six months. It allowed visitors from the West to visit the GDR for up to 30 days a year, at first for one day at a time, later for two. On principle, visitors had to leave by the same crossing point which they had used for entry. This opportunity was used relatively often by West Germans living close to the border. Applications by East Germans in a similar situation were however dealt with restrictively, and it was mostly GDR pensioners who were able to use the local border traffic regulation to any considerable degree.

Blocking of the transit route to Lauenburg (West Germany) by GDR border guards, Heerstrasse control point, Berlin, Staaken district, 5 March 1969 (Photo: Landesarchiv Berlin)

In spite of hassle on the part of the "GDR border control organs", and notwithstanding the compulsory exchange of deutschmarks for East German marks, six to seven million West Germans and West Berliners visited the GDR each year. Most of them had family ties, and when they got there, they talked about their lives. Not only their information, but their mere presence, demonstrated a lifestyle which in itself contradicted the mantra-like assertions of the GDR leadership that "capitalism in the FRG" was on its last legs, and that its death-throes manifested themselves in particularly aggressive behaviour.

In order to enter the GDR, West Germans needed an entry visa issued by the GDR, while West Berliners had to fill out a special application form. In addition to the "local border traffic" agreed in 1971, and the day-visa permitting West Germans to enter via West Berlin, it was above all the biannual International Leipzig Fair that provided an uncomplicated opportunity for Westerners to visit the GDR. The Fair Ticket available in the West allowed Westerners to stay in the Leipzig re-

Reisende
in das
Bundesgebiet

Nach dem Transitabkommen
sind bestimmte Vorschriften der DDR
zu beachten, u. a.

- kein Material verbreiten
- keine Personen aufnehmen
- die Transitwege nicht verlassen
- Strafvorschriften
  und die Straßenverkehrsvorschriften
  der DDR beachten!

Einzelheiten
in dem hier erhältlichen Merkblatt

Notice for transit travellers, Heerstrasse control point (crossing-point for transit traffic to West Berlin) Berlin, Spandau district, 27 November 1973 (Photo: Landesarchiv Berlin/Karl-Heinz Schubert)

gion and in designated hotels in neighbouring regions. Tourist trips to the GDR by West Germans and West Berliners could be booked from their local travel agents, and particularly in the 1970s and 80s, West German school students and other young people had the chance to undertake educational trips to the East booked through GDR travel agents. While these offers were taken up to a certain degree, young West Germans had meanwhile discovered the world to the west of Germany. Trips to Paris or London were more popular than time-consuming border controls, the sight of decaying GDR towns, and a limited range of goods in the shops, which were in any case of little interest to young people from the West. In the late 1980s, a few selected and carefully vetted young East Germans were also permitted to visit Western countries, including the Federal Republic, on trips organized by the GDR state travel office "Jugendtourist".

Hundreds of thousands of GDR pensioners, allowed to travel once a year to West Germany and West Berlin, contributed, with their tales and particularly through the longingly awaited presents from the "West", to an image of an inaccessible, distant world. Chewing gum, chocolate, cigarettes, real coffee, Matchbox toy cars, felt-tip pens, jeans and nylon shirts put across a simplified picture of a different society. The notion that the grass in the West was greener and the sky bluer was dismissed with a smile of disbelief by many of those who stayed at home, but matched the dreams of many in the East. The tales of often humiliating border controls in the GDR and the heavy hearts of all travellers from East or West shortly before crossing the border also helped to characterize the image of the GDR in the eyes of many younger people in both halves of Germany.

Only in exceptional cases were East German pensioners, or the few others allowed to travel, permitted to use their own cars to get to West Germany or West Berlin. The most common form of transport to the West was the railway. The high-security rail-stations in the restricted border area resembled fortresses. A dense network of GDR border troops with an officer in command, together with customs officials, worked side-by-side with the railway staff day and night. Checks on passengers, railway workers and other people, as well as on goods and vehicles, were however carried out by members of the passport control units of the Ministry of State Security (Stasi), who wore the uniform of the border guards. The members of this Stasi unit were given special training not only initially but on an ongoing basis, and it was they who determined procedures at the stations on the border and all other crossing-points to West Germany and West Berlin, in spite of the fact that formally, the border-

Autobahn towards Helmstedt (West Germany); Easter traffic from West Berlin (behind the Dreilinden control point). In the background, left: Soviet Tank Memorial and border installations,11 April 1974 (Photo: Landesarchiv Berlin)

guard officers were higher in rank. In any case escape via the rail network was virtually impossible thanks to not only a multitude of internal regulations, but also to a technical system perfected since 1966 by the Deutsche Reichsbahn (the East German railway system, which, curiously, had retained the pre-war name). Even West German transit passengers travelling between West Germany and West Berlin, who normally only had to show a passport or ID card in the train, were affected by the stifling atmosphere in the GDR stations on the border. The formal "We welcome you to the German Democratic Republic" which blared out over the tinny loudspeakers at the border stations could not dispel the spookiness of the experience, which was characterized by uniformed armed men, dogs, barbed wire, fences, walls and watchtowers. Quite apart from the stations on the inner-German border, such as Oebisfelde, Marienborn, Gerstungen and Probstzella, Friedrichstrasse station in East Berlin was a particular curiosity of the situation in divided Germany. Even before the Wall was built, internal GDR rail traffic terminated at Friedrichstrasse, and did not cross West Berlin territory. Immediately after 13 August 1961, the former railway junction at the heart of a world metropolis, which also served the local overhead and underground rail networks, became an elaborately secured interface in inner-German rail traffic. Unlike the other stations on the border between East and West, the Friedrichstrasse crossing-point consisted of two zones blocked off from each other, separating East and West. The station itself, it should be noted, stood entirely within the territory of East Berlin – the Wall was 1500 metres to the west. The underground area, with the stops for the local Berlin city trains, was open only to passengers using the West Berlin public transport services, for which it was an interchange station between different lines.

This station, on the West Berlin rail network, but in East Berlin, also provided travellers with the chance to buy duty-free goods at the "Intershops" operated by the GDR, which encouraged shoppers from West Berlin to come simply for that purpose, without having to pass a crossing-point to do so. The passage connecting the two city rail networks (the U-Bahn or underground, and the S-Bahn, largely overhead) also provided a link for station officials with special permits to pass between the Eastern and Western zones of the station. At the same time, these crossings were also used for smuggling spies and other similarly legitimated individuals. For example in 1976 and 1978 members of the West German terrorist group, the Red Army Faction (also known as the Baader-Meinhof group), wanted by the police in West Germany, used this route to enter East Germany. The overground part of the station was secured by a three-metre-high

Friedrichstrasse Station crossing-point, Berlin, Mitte district,
Christmas Day 1974 (Photo: Landesarchiv Berlin)

Notice in Friedrich-
strasse station
(Eastern section),
Berlin, Mitte dis-
trict, April 1985
(Photo: Wolfgang
Kramer)

barrier of wire-reinforced glass, which in 1982 was replaced by a ceiling-high steel wall. This wall separated the zone used by the S-Bahn to the West from the
platform serving East Berlin travellers – in their case,
the end of the road. A maze of passages, staircases and
suites of rooms led via a mezzanine storey to the border-control rooms, monitored by 140 video cameras.
Those with the required passports and paperwork
were conducted through three passport controls and
the customs inspection before reaching the other half
of the station. For those going from East to West, it

Brandenburg Gate (Brandenburger Tor). In the background: The Berlin Wall, Pariser Platz. In the foreground: Unter den Linden, 9 May 1987 (Photo: Landesarchiv Berlin/Günter Schneider)

was only after the train had left the platform that it became clear that they really would be in West Berlin in a couple of minutes. In 1962 a – by the standards of

the time – modern addition to Friedrichstrasse station was built for border-control purposes: it was popularly known as the "palace of tears". The trains provided by the GDR for the transit routes from West
Berlin to West Germany were parked on special sid-

Drewitz-Dreilinden crossing-point, Potsdam/Berlin, 31 March 1972 (Photo: Bundesarchiv Koblenz/ADN ZB, Hartmut Reiche, 183-L0331-0005)

Crossing-point between East Staaken (in West Berlin, Spandau district) and Potsdam region (GDR), 1988 (Photo: Wolfgang Kramer)

Above and below: Bornholmer Strasse crossing-point, Berlin, Kreuzberg district, 1988 (Photo: Wolfgang Kramer)

ings in the city's Rummelsburg district. Here they were cleaned, serviced and above all laboriously inspected, in order to prevent any escape by GDR citizens. Transferred (without stopping) as far as Friedrichstrasse with securely locked doors, and under the surveillance of the transport police, they were then opened (in the "Western" zone of the station) to provide ingress for transit passengers from West Berlin. On GDR territory, all transit trains had absolute priority, and were only allowed to stop in exceptional cases. Transit passengers were not allowed to alight at the border stations on the GDR side.

Alongside the stations on the border, it was the road crossing-points, nearly all of them on motorways, that formed the main official means of getting across the inner-German border. These crossing-points were used predominantly by travellers using the transit routes between West Germany and West Berlin. For those still far from the border on the Eastern side, they were unmistakable as highly-secured, monstrous installations in the restricted zone. One of the most-used motorway crossing-points was Hirschberg/Rudolphstein on the A9 motorway, the main traffic artery between Berlin and Nuremberg/Munich. Opened in 1966, it remained in existence until 1990.

Travellers coming from Berlin and bound for Bavaria were informed as far back as the Schleiz junction that this was the final exit before the border. For GDR citizens, this meant that they could proceed no further, even though there was still more than 20 kilometres of motorway on GDR territory between them and the border. Then, on the motorway near the village of Blintendorf, the People's Police stopped drivers to see whether they were authorized to proceed. Here at the latest, GDR citizens without valid permits for a journey to the West were conducted off the motorway. West Berliners and West Germans, plus those few East Germans with a permit, were then confronted a few

Oberbaum Bridge crossing-point, Berlin, Kreuzberg (West) and Friedrichshain (East) districts, 1988 (Photo: Wolfgang Kramer)

kilometres further on by the large grey installation that constituted the Hirschberg/Rudolphstein crossing-point, with its extensive system of control points along with devices to prevent anyone seeking to cross by brute force. These latter included barriers of steel and concrete let into the carriageway. Travellers first had to surrender their documents at a preliminary control post; provided there was no irregularity, these were normally returned at a further point down the line. The documents were checked by the Stasi passport-control unit. If no further checks were carried out, for example by customs, then the travellers finally reached Bavarian soil. In the 1980s, the modern service area with its cafeteria on a bridge over the motorway shortly beyond the border was, so to speak, the visual gateway to the West. For many West Berliners, the Franconian countryside which they now entered was one of the most popular and accessible holiday regions beyond the inner-German border, a fact which provided an economic shot in the arm for parts of this region in the 1970s and 80s.

On the transit routes through the GDR, West Berliners and West Germans were permitted to use the few motorway service areas, like for example the ones at Michendorf or the Hermsdorf intersection. Here too, from the 1970s, there were East German "Intershops", where goods could be bought for deutschmarks and other Western currencies. The service areas also provided a chance of a "secret" rendezvous with friends and relations from the GDR, although it goes without saying that these took place under the eyes of the Stasi. In the 1980s, a few stopping places were also set up along GDR motorways for the exclusive use of transit drivers and passengers. These stopping places, such as Rodaborn in Thuringia, were closed to GDR citizens. All services, e.g. use of the toilets, had to be paid for in deutschmarks or other hard currency, thus helping to top up the GDR's scanty reserves. Transit drivers were forbidden on principle to leave the transit route through the GDR.

In spite of the opportunities to secretly meet friends and relations at the motorway service areas on the transit routes through the GDR, or to visit the GDR, many West Germans and West Berliners were unable to make use of them. Until well into the 1980s, this group included above all anyone who had left the GDR legally or illegally since 1961. This group were often refused entry to the GDR, and in some cases former GDR citizens had to reckon on the possibility of arrest if they set foot on GDR soil. Although the

Rendezvous 10 years after the building of the Wall: secret meeting at the Hermsdorfer intersection (Thuringia). Two sisters with families from West Berlin and the GDR, 1971 (Photo: Führ)

GDR leadership relaxed these conditions in 1972, a less complicated means of personal contact with friends and relations was to meet in another of the communist countries to which GDR citizens were allowed to travel. Particularly popular venues for such meetings were the cities of Prague and Budapest, or Lake Balaton in Hungary, where friends and relations from East and West could take holidays together.

On 17 October 1973 the head of the People's Police issued an "Order relating to travel by the citizens of the GDR". This order, and Order no. 2 relating to travel dated 14 June 1973, laid down the legal framework for possibilities of travel by GDR citizens to the "non-socialist states" and West Berlin for the next ten years. For the first time, others besides pensioners and the privileged "travel cadres" were allowed to make an application for travel "in urgent family circumstances". These were deemed to include births, marriages, silver, golden and diamond weddings, 65th and 70th wedding anniversaries, life-threatening illnesses, and deaths. The appropriate documentation had to be obtained from West German authorities, and hence by those family members living in the Federal Republic, and sent to the GDR. The application for the journey itself, however, had to be made at a People's Police office in the GDR by the travellers themselves, who had to be grandparents, parents, children or siblings (including half-siblings) of the family member in the West whose circumstances occasioned the meeting. This order was accompanied until 1989 by 57 internal guidelines for the passport and registration officials of the People's Police, designed to regulate how this legal stipulation was to be implemented. These officials were for example told to conduct an interview with the applicants in which their private lives, their work and their "social activity" would be discussed. The guidelines particularly stressed that the "bonds with the GDR" and the personal situation of the applicant were to be central when deciding whether to grant or refuse an application. The basis for the permit procedure was informal approval by the "state superiors" (i.e. managers) at the place of work and an enquiry at the local office (Abschnittsbevollmächtigter – ABV) of the People's Police. All the applications were automatically forwarded to the local office of the Stasi, whose members could overturn positive decisions by the local People's Police if the applicant did not fit into a prescribed mould. If the application was rejected, no explanation on the part of the People's Police would be forthcoming.

Should a successful applicant not return after the family visit to West Germany, West Berlin or non-communist third country, there would be an intensive epilogue in the office which had granted the application. First of all, the former citizen of the GDR would be formally charged under section 213 of the criminal code (illegal border crossing), although such charges were usually dropped. The offence would be noted, and the culprit banned from returning to the GDR for an undefined period. His or her relations would not normally succeed in subsequent applications.

"10. Principles for examining and deciding on applications to cross the state border of the GDR
10.1. General principles
10.1.1. Decisions on travel applications are political decisions, which demand a high degree of vigilance and must be taken in accordance with the security interests of the GDR.
When deciding on applications, the purpose of the journey must be borne in mind first and foremost. The officer must decide whether the applicant provides sufficient assurance of behaving in a proper manner outside the GDR, or, as the case may be, his sojourn in the GDR does not run counter to the interests of our state."

Directive issued to officers of the People's Police in the GDR 40/1974

In the "Order relating to regulations concerning travel by citizens of the GDR" dated 15 February 1982, the definition of "urgent family circumstance" was extended to include "Jugendweihe" (the East German adolescent rite-of-passage ceremony), confirmation, first communion and certain birthdays (60th, 65th, 70th, 75th and every subsequent birthday). This order, the penultimate relating to travel in the history of the GDR, remained in force until 31 December 1988, and led to an explosion in travel related to "urgent family circumstances" by GDR citizens living behind what was otherwise a hermetically sealed border. Thus in 1987 in the Magdeburg region alone, more than 90,000 travel applications in urgent family circumstances were granted, and in the first six months of 1988 already more than 52,000. At that time, the region was home to 1.25 million people. In the same period, 7,000 applications were not accepted, and 8,000 refused. But this still means that 83.2% of the travel applications in this region were approved. Of those whose applications in the Magdeburg region were granted in the first half of 1988, only 92, i.e. 0.18%, did not return. As there was, until 31 December 1988, no right of appeal to a court of law against a rejection of an application by a People's Police district office, there was little recourse in such a situation. Particularly in the 1980s, however, rejected applicants made use of the right to administrative review at various official levels going right up to the party boss and head of state. Thus in 1987 in the Magdeburg region 2,147 such requests for review were registered, a figure which more than doubled the following year. However only one in ten of such reviews resulted in a positive outcome for the applicant.

On 30 November 1988 the "Order relating to foreign travel by citizens of the German Democratic Republic" was issued; it came into force on 1 January 1989. This was the last such set of travel regulations to be issued before the fall of the Berlin Wall and the inner-German border. It was ultimately due to the pressure of the enormous increase in the number of applications for exit visas in the GDR and the general mood amongst large sections of the population. Among the new features were the possibility of acquiring a GDR passport without a specific reason, the consolidation of all travel categories including permanent departure from the GDR, the extension of the category of persons permitted to make an application, and above all the possibility of learning why an application had been refused, with a legal right to appeal. This final order relating to travel unleashed a flood of applications to visit West Germany and West Berlin: it was the final safety-valve of a state on its last legs, but was opened too late.

During the period when Germany was divided, family contacts and friendships formed an important ba-

GDR postage stamp, 25th anniversary of the building of the Wall, 1986 (Photo: Führ)

sis for an ongoing feeling of a common German nationhood, and a firm cross-border foundation. Already from 1952, family meetings across the border were only possible to a limited degree. Only West Germans and West Berliners could visit the GDR without serious problems, not the other way about. Until August 1961, access to West Berlin by East Berliners and East Germans was possible virtually without restriction. And until 1961 there was also the possibility for GDR citizens to travel to West Germany on business, for congresses, for further vocational training, sporting competitions or other events.

The precondition was an appropriate application approved by the GDR authorities. Stable contacts among family and friends in East and West existed above all via the postal services. News was exchanged by letter and postcard. Photographs were sent, and from time to time deutschmarks were sent to the East. Word soon got around that the GDR authorities were not respecting the confidentiality of the mail, and in many cases it was reported that money had been removed from the envelope. In spite of the border, numerous new cross-border pen-friendships developed, often organized by church groups. Hobbies in common, for example philately, popular in both halves of Germany, led to contacts for the purpose of exchanging stamps, and these in turn could lead to closer friendships. GDR philatelists mostly collected West German and West Berlin stamps, and vice versa. Joint sports events and competitions, not least involving small clubs, linked people in both German states in spite of the border, and in the 1950s were part of the everyday East-West relationship. However, the attempt by GDR sports functionaries to exploit sporting events between clubs on either side of the border for political ends led to temporary setbacks. After the building of the Berlin Wall in 1961, the number of sporting encounters sank to a minimum. Only in high-performance sport did the GDR leadership succeed in misusing sport to represent the struggle between the systems. The "GDR diplomats in track-suits" however, in the Olympic Games of 1956, 1960, 1964 and 1968, had to demonstrate their prowess alongside West German sportsmen and -women in a united German team. It was in 1968 that the International Olympic Committee finally recognized the National Olympic Committee of the GDR, so that the two German states were each represented with a team of their own. High-performance sport, particularly promoted by the state, was the GDR's self-advertisement to the world in the 1970s and 80s. Private contacts with West German sportsmen and -women were however not looked upon kindly, and the GDR leadership reacted with particular sensitivity when renowned sports personalities, who had been provided with every encouragement and inducement, did not return from sports events in the West.

The successes of the GDR in the sporting field certainly strengthened the feeling of identity among a section of the population, but that didn't stop the many sports enthusiasts in the GDR from taking a lively interest in West German sport. Thus workers at the machines in "People's Own Factories" were often better informed about the soccer results in the (West German) Bundesliga than about the soccer being played in the GDR equivalent. Radio listeners and TV viewers would cheer the successes of West German sportsmen, women and teams, just as would the spectators at sports events in the GDR where West Germans were competing.

It was not just the sporting events in the West that were followed on the radio (not least on the modern portable radios then gaining in popularity) and on TV in the East. These electronic media were to become the crucial link in divided Germany. The airwaves of broadcasters from Western Europe and West Berlin did not stop at state borders, not even one so well fortified as that of the GDR. The massive propaganda campaign waged by the state and party leadership in the 1950s and 60s in particular against the reception of Western radio and TV programmes had no more effect than attempted jamming, prohibitions, or the notorious "Operation Ochsenkopf" in the autumn of 1961. This latter involved members of the "Free German Youth" (the official GDR youth organization) destroying private aerials oriented towards the TV transmitter on the Ochsenkopf, a mountain in Bavaria not far from where the inner-German and Czech borders met. The centralized, censored state media landscape in the GDR had little to offer alongside the varied services provided by the Western broadcasters. It is true that some GDR programmes were watched in East and West alike, but ratings were often rock-bottom.

A particularly important role was played by Western radio stations, which played current West European and American music. Broadcasters such as Radio Luxembourg, the BBC, Deutschlandfunk (a nationwide broadcaster based in Cologne) or Saarländischer Rundfunk (based in the Saar), using simple medium or long-wave transmitters, were just as popular as the modern FM technology of Norddeutscher Rundfunk (Hamburg), the Sender Freies Berlin (SFB), or that particular bugbear of the GDR authorities, the likewise Berlin-based Rundfunk im Amerikanischen Sektor (RIAS). The international Western music culture,

which even in the West was the expression of a totally different outlook on life on the part of the younger
generation in particular, became the most important
cross-border cultural input for the post-war generation in the GDR as they reached adolescence. The cultural image of most young East Germans was largely
moulded by rock´n'roll and other styles of pop music
from the 60s to the 80s, not to mention that charac-
teristically West German musical phenomenon, the
"Schlager". Whether it was entertainment or news,
political journalism, sports programmes or detective
films, the media dominance of the West on East German soil was a fact that could not be ignored. For
many GDR citizens this led to the typical phenomenon
of a life in two worlds: at the workplace or when shopping, the real world of the GDR, and in the evening,
notwithstanding the Wall and the barbed wire, the
Western world as filtered through the Western media.

Cultural exchange between the two German states,
still characterized by a degree of normalcy in the
1950s, and kept alive in various joint official projects
as well as by lively private or church contacts, saw a
marked decline following the building of the Berlin
Wall, and did not start to recover until the 1970s and
80s. Prominent GDR artists and other "Kulturschaf-
fende" ("culture-creators") were in a few cases allowed once more to appear or work in West Germany
or West Berlin from the 1970s, while some were even
issued with a semi-permanent visa to live in the Federal Republic. In the 1980s in particular, Western
artists performed at concerts and other events in the
GDR. West German artists who expressed attitudes
critical of the GDR were however rewarded by the
latter with a performance ban. Collaboration between
museums, in the theatrical world, between writers' associations and in the spheres of music and film led to
official contacts and to joint work between East and

20 years of Rias ("Radio In the American Sector"), event in the Deutschlandhalle in West Berlin, 26 February 1966 (Photo: Landesarchiv Berlin/Karl-Heinz Schubert)

West. In 1976, the critical chansonnier Wolf Biermann was stripped of his GDR citizenship while on a concert tour in West Germany; this had far-reaching consequences for culture in the GDR. Hitherto, he had been known only to a restricted circle of intellectuals and artists in the GDR, but the action of the GDR authorities made him a celebrity overnight. Alongside all the usual forms of harassment, the GDR leadership had evidently pulled a final stop: they no longer imprisoned their citizens behind a border, but dumped those they did not like by decree. The subsequent exodus of prominent GDR artists to the West, such as actress Angelica Domröse, actor, singer and writer Manfred Krug, and writers Sarah Kirsch and Günter Kunert, attracted huge public attention in the GDR. People who had hitherto been generally well-disposed towards the GDR system now came to have substantial doubts regarding "their" state. In 1986 the two states put their names to a binding agreement on short and medium-term goals of cultural co-operation between them. This put an end to the seemingly random nature of cultural collaboration, largely caused by the inconstancy of the GDR in this field, but apart from this agreement, there were few additional cultural bonuses in the final years of divided Germany. A particular role in the lives of the citizens of the GDR was played by the "parcel from the West". While in the 1950s and 60s these parcels largely contained foodstuffs such as butter or legumes, or so-called luxuries such as cigarettes, chewing-gum, chocolate, coffee or cocoa, from the 1970s the "Westpaket" increasingly came to mean a broader spectrum of West German goodies. Particularly popular in the GDR were above all fashion items such as jeans or tights, cosmetics and

Poster displayed in West German post offices: "Your parcel for 'over there': they are waiting for it. Information at the counter." 1950s/60s (Photo: Führ)

Newly erected telephone boxes by the sector boundary in West Berlin at the Brandenburg Gate, Tiergarten district, Strasse des 17. Juni, 23 December 1959 (Photo: Landesarchiv Berlin/Gert Schütz)

articles of personal hygiene, toys, baking ingredients, and tropical fruits, all of which were hard to come by in the planned economy of the East. Sought-after recordings of modern music, along with books and magazines, were only permitted by the GDR author-ities to a limited degree, and often, mostly without any reason being given, confiscated by the customs. Parcels were an important economic factor for many East Germans lucky enough to have friends or rela-tives in the West. This circumstance was ultimately factored into their calculations by the GDR leader-ship. In particular the West German churches and many of their parishioners endeavoured to relieve hardships in their sister parishes in the GDR. In re-turn, the people in the East sent parcels to the West, particularly at Christmas, with contents compiled from the very restricted range on offer, and often at con-siderable expense.

While in the 1950s and 60s telephone calls between most places in the East and the West had to be connected by an operator, subscriber trunk dialling via a network covering both parts of Germany developed only sluggishly. As before the fall of the Wall in 1989 only a small proportion of GDR inhabitants had a private telephone, calls were in any case only possible to a limited extent. Even then, a "click" in the line would signal to both speakers that their conversation in many cases involved a third party. Various groups of people, such as members of the armed forces and higher-ranking public officials, on both sides of the border, were in any case not allowed contacts with the other side. By 1986, finally, subscribers on 1,106 of the 1,500 local GDR exchanges were able to dial West German numbers direct.

In Western Europe since the 1950s, the system of "twinning" between towns in different countries had developed into a form of international co-operation at local level, leading to more-or-less stable cross-border partnerships. These twinning arrangements relied on the commitment of those on both (or all) sides. The young Federal Republic had, in this period, oriented itself predominantly to Western Europe in this respect, mostly France. A contractual twinning arrangement with a town in the GDR would have amounted to a kind of recognition of the GDR as a separate state, and was thus not on the cards. Only after the huge political change brought about by the government coalition of Social Democrats and Free Democrats under Willy Brandt in the early 1970s was there a change of heart in this area. Requests on the part of the West German towns to twin with counterparts in the GDR were however either rejected or left unanswered.

Not until 25 April 1986 was a twinning agreement signed – between Saarlouis in the Saarland and Eisenhüttenstadt, close to the Polish border. It had been preceded by talks between the East German leader Erich Honecker, a native of the Saarland, and the then state premier of the Saarland, Oskar Lafontaine. This opened the way for a flood of applications for inner-German twinning arrangements. On the GDR side, however, the choice of twin town was often influenced in incomprehensible ways, and of course the proposed arrangement was worked out down to the last detail. Spontaneous relationships, like travel possibilities for the average GDR citizen, were virtually impossible in the context of these twinning arrangements. Thus the delegations on the GDR side consisted mostly of apparatchiks and state officials.

"We Germans are one people and one nation. We feel that we belong together because we share the same history. We experienced 8 May 1945 as the common fate of our people. We feel we belong together in our desire for peace. The German soil of both states should emanate peace and good-neighbourliness with all countries. Nor should others make it a danger to peace. People in Germany are united in wanting a peace that includes justice and human rights for all nations, including ours. It is not a Europe of walls that can create cross-border reconciliation, but rather a continent which deprives its border of their divisive aspect."

Richard von Weizsäcker, President of the
Federal Republic of Germany
on 8 May 1985 (the 40th anniversary of
Germany's surrender) in the Bundestag

FLIGHT, EMIGRATION AND TRAVEL FROM EAST TO WEST

During the almost 41 years of its existence, some 3.8 million people left the GDR. This is more people than live in the federal capital, Berlin, and only slightly fewer than live in eastern Germany's most populous state, Saxony. Most of these people, many of whom had to leave all their belongings behind, left "illegally" and after 1957 risked prosecution for the offence of "flight from the republic". While this migration was until 1952 still possible across almost all the sections of the inner-German border and the border around Berlin, most "flights" until 13 August 1961 were across the open border between the Soviet and Western sectors in Berlin, and most refugees used the Berlin local rail networks for the purpose. People talked about "going across" or "clearing out".

Pensioners and invalids in the GDR were the only group who could, virtually throughout the period of its existence, leave the state with official permission. By doing so, of course, they relieved the communist state of the need to pay their pension, while also freeing up the housing market, accommodation in the GDR being in short supply. Finally, in the 1970s and 80s, numerous mostly young people turned their backs on the GDR after putting in an "exit application". Time and again, and not always successfully, people from the GDR sought to escape across the lethal border installations. From late summer 1989, hundreds of thousands left the GDR via third countries such as Czechoslovakia and Hungary. Between the fall of the Wall and the abolition of the inner-German border following 9 November 1989, and formal re-unification on 3 October 1990, hundreds of thousands more made the journey to the West.

Marienfelde Emergency Reception Camp, Berlin, Tempelhof district, Marienfelder Allee, 4 September 1958 (Photo: Landesarchiv Berlin/Gert Schütz)

It cannot be said that there was any one reason for leaving. Most GDR citizens were looking for a better standard of living and saw in the West German system above all the glitter of the social market economy, most clearly symbolized by the "economic miracle" of the 1950s and 60s. A major role was also played by dissatisfaction with political conditions in the GDR, in a system imposed on the country from the outside when the USSR, as one of the occupying powers, sought to import its own ideology. It was a system that led to people increasingly having their decisions made for them, characterized by restrictions on personal freedom, to the pervasion of ideology in all areas of life, and by repressive measures on the part of the state. The agitation and propaganda carried on by the GDR was particularly counterproductive, as in most cases it had nothing to do with reality. Of course, family was another important motive for moving to West Germany or West Berlin. In this context, there were also moves from West to East, just as there were of course people who wanted to escape the general legislation of the state in which they lived. It should not be forgotten that during the period of division, some half-million Germans left the Western occupation zones and later the Federal Republic for the Soviet Zone and the GDR. The high points of the wave of refugees from East to West were 1953, following the events of 17 June of that year, when 331,390 people left the GDR, 1956 with 279,189 officially registered border-crossers, and 1961, when by mid-year already 159,730 had left. Almost half of the inner-German migrants were under 25.

The great majority of refugees, expellees and re-settlers, including the millions of Germans from what had formerly been German territory in the East, had first to pass through transit camps in the British and American zones, while in the Soviet zone they were directly integrated via local institutions. Few refugees were registered in the French zone in the immediate post-war period. It should be noted that of those coming from Germany's lost eastern territories, a quarter chose to remain in the Soviet zone, where, with political discretion, they were known as "Umsiedler" or "re-settlers". In the West, they were termed "Vertriebene" ("expellees") or "Ostflüchtlinge" ("refugees from the east"). Some of these later moved on to the West. Those leaving the Soviet zone for the West also had to pass through the transit camps if they could not be put up by friends or relations.

After the foundation of the two German states in 1949, an emergency reception procedure regulated the legal and social integration of refugees from the GDR. This procedure was enshrined in the Federal Republic's Emergency Reception Law of 22 August 1950. Reception committees had to question the refugees and decide whether there were grounds for according them a permit to remain in West Germany.

Process-slip for the emergency reception procedure at the Marienfelde Emergency Reception Camp, Berlin, January 1961 (Photo: Führ)

Among the grounds for acceptance were political reasons, danger to life and limb, or proven restriction of freedom. Even when these reasons were absent, refugees from the GDR itself could stay, since under West German law they were German citizens; they did not however receive any financial benefits. In West Berlin, where most refugees and re-settlers arrived, the emergency reception camp in Marienfelde became the central location for most emergency reception procedures on 14 April 1953, and retained this status until 1989. The procedure comprised 13 stages and also included a medical examination. A special feature in West Berlin was the interrogation of male applicants by the three Western Allies. If the outcome was positive, most of the new arrivals were flown on to West Germany, and distributed among the various states under a quota system. The emergency reception camp in Giessen (from 1950) was the central transit venue for GDR refugees in the Federal Republic. The majority of those who fled via Hungary and Austria, and those who emigrated to the West following the occupations of the West German embassies in Warsaw, Prague and Budapest in the summer of 1989 underwent the emergency reception procedure here. After the inner-German border was opened, this was also the camp which experienced the greatest flood of GDR applicants.

A particular chapter was formed by the numerous escape stories reflecting audacity, imagination, despair, inventiveness, good fortune and also dreadful misfortune. Since the closure of the inner-German border in 1952, crossing the former "green" border had become a difficult undertaking, even though the opportunities for flight to the West were still fairly numerous. The flight of a large proportion of the villagers of Bösekendorf to Lower Saxony at various intervals aroused public attention well beyond the confines of the region. As early as July 1952, three families moved across the border with their livestock. After the building of the Wall in Berlin and further tightening of security on the inner-German border, a group of 53 villagers finally succeeded in October 1961 in escaping with a horse-cart. Each of the refugees was allowed to carry one sack with his or her belongings, behind which the women and children of the 14 families concealed themselves. The mass escape was not noticed at first, and the party arrived safely in Lower Saxony. In February 1963 a further group of twelve villagers, led by an NCO of the border guard, succeeded in negotiating the minefield which had been laid in the meantime.

While between the closure of the border in Berlin on 13 August and the end of the year, 8,507 people still succeeded in getting across, that number had dropped by 1966 to a total of just 1,736 (including both the inner-German and Berlin borders). The increasingly per-

A group of refugees overcome the border installations between Pankow (East Berlin) and Reinickendorf (West Berlin). According to the photographer, the group were expected in the West; the GDR border guards did not intervene. September 1961 (Photo: ullstein bild – Männling)

fect technology of the border installations, improved training and organization of the border guards, and co-operation between the People's Police and volunteers in the hinterland of the border played a not insignificant role. An internal GDR secret memorandum, titled "Overview of attempted and successful border violations across the border security installations (1 Dec 74 – 31 May 82)" makes for interesting reading. Thus 7,282 arrests of "border violators" were registered in this period, 5,882 by the People's Police and 1,087 by the border guards. According to the figures in this document, only 313 refugees from the GDR succeeded in crossing the border during this time.

In the first few weeks after the sealing of the Berlin sector boundary, many people still attempted the direct way across the as yet provisional barriers – through barbed-wire entanglements, over simple fences and across the city's waterways. Every such attempt, however, led to an increase in security on that section of the border, irrespective of the general strengthening of the installations. Spectacular, and quickly disseminated by the international media, were the dramatic escapes by Berlin citizens from the windows of their houses and flats where the outside walls stood directly on the sector border (ill. pp. 64/65). Film recordings in particular gave wide coverage to leaps by women and men from various storeys of their houses, e.g. in Bernauer Strasse, shortly after the border was closed. The West Berlin public and authorities alike sought to help people whose lives were endangered by these attempts, for example by holding out rescue nets (ill. p. 63).

In Berlin it was only a few months after a start was made on building the Wall that the great age of the tunnellers began. Mostly in spectacular fashion, quite large groups of people were able to flee to the West in this way. As early as January 1962 the first great tunnel escape succeeded, with 28 people emerging into the daylight in the Oranienburger Chaussee. Further elaborate tunnel digs from East to West followed, and ultimately things were speeded up by others digging from West to East.

The most spectacular case of all was a tunnel more than 150 metres long from Bernauer Strasse in West Berlin beneath a building in Schönholzer Strasse in the Soviet sector. At times, more than 40 helpers were working round the clock on this tunnel, with the professionalism of experienced miners. After many difficulties, at the beginning of September 1962 the undertaking was complete. On 14 September, 29 people, including two babies, reached the West amidst tears of joy, filmed live by the American TV company NBC, which had been let in on the secret and had, so to speak, sponsored the enterprise. The US television reports were accompanied by emotional pictures, and exposed the inhumanity of the GDR's border regime

A picture that went round the world! Warrant Officer Conrad Schumann, on duty as a guard on Bernauer Strasse in Berlin, leaps across the barbed wire between Mitte (East) and Wedding (West) districts, 15 August 1961 (Photo: ullstein bild – Peter Leibing)

for all to see. Soon the West German media and private backers also started providing massive financial support for those tunnelling beneath the sector boundary. One of the busiest tunnel-builders was a West Berliner named Wolfgang Fuchs (1939–2001), who became known in the media as the "tunnel fox" (a pun on his name) and with the aid of students from West Berlin's Technical University, had numerous escape tunnels built. Increasingly the border guards, the Stasi and the People's Police stepped up their efforts to prevent this tunnelling activity. Finally, after an escape tunnel in Strelitzer Strasse was discovered by GDR border guards, there was an exchange of fire between the soldiers and the West Berlin escape helpers, resulting in the death of the GDR border guard Egon Schultz (1943–1964). An NCO, and soon fêted as a martyr in the still young tradition of the border guards, he had in fact been the victim of "friendly fire". Thus Schultz became one of the first fatalities among the soldiers on border duty. This exchange of fire ended the great age of the tunnel-builders: for the financial backers, the business had become too dangerous.

Money however was to play an increasingly important role in planning escapes from the GDR. As border security was intensified, the possibilities of getting across diminished. Professional Western "escape helpers" developed increasingly sophisticated strategies to enable GDR citizens to get to the West. In the 1960s and 70s, one notable method was the use of specially prepared vehicles on the transit routes to and from Berlin. However every time the GDR authorities made an arrest, this led to intensification of controls on the inner-German border. Not only the refugees themselves, but any escape-helpers who got arrested, could reckon on long terms of imprisonment in the GDR. The

East Berlin, S-Bahn station Wollankstrasse, escape tunnel, 1 February 1962 (Photo: Bundesarchiv Koblenz, 183-90157-0001)

Watchtower at the Griebnitzsee, Potsdam-Babelsberg, border to West-Berlin (Zehlendorf), photo from East to West, c. 1975 (Photo: Führ)

Stasi also liked to point to those GDR citizens who lost their lives while trying to escape in technically defective vehicles. Until well into the 1980s, the Stasi prepared documentations, sometimes in the form of touring exhibitions, designed to deter GDR citizens by presenting these examples. Even in the late 1960s, the high risk run by the escape-helpers meant that an escape attempt might cost up to 20,000 deutschmarks. These costs were often borne by close relatives or friends of the refugee in the West.

Sometimes the refugee was under contract to work off the debt once he or she had successfully arrived in the West. One popular form of organized escape-help was the passing-on of "lost" passports of citizens of Western European countries by the helper. A number of East Germans used this method to get to the West via neighbouring communist countries. Direct flight across the borders of Hungary or Czechoslovakia was almost impossible, as the borders of these countries with West Germany, Austria, Turkey and Yugoslavia were heavily fortified and above all adequately secured by the border units of the "fraternal country" concerned.

Until the late 1980s, any East Germans arrested in the border areas of Czechoslovakia, Hungary or Bulgaria were deported to the GDR, where they had to reckon with a prison term. It was only with the headlong political changes of the late 1980s, resulting from perestroika in the USSR and a change of heart on the part of the political leadership in various communist countries, that in the second half of 1989 the strict border regime in Hungary and Czechoslovakia was dropped, and East Germans were also among the beneficiaries. A pioneer role was played by the Hungarian government, which as early as 2 May 1989 started dismantling its border installations. After more than 3,000 GDR citizens fled to Austria via Hungary in August of that year, the Hungarians finally opened their borders with the West on 10/11 September. Within three days, more than 15,000 GDR citizens took this opportunity to leave.

Time and again, vehicles of all kinds were used to break through the inner-German border or the Berlin Wall. Particularly spectacular was the journey of a complete railway train from Oranienburg to West Berlin on 5 December 1961, with 26 people on board. Likewise by rail, eight pupils of an East Berlin high school fled at the beginning of 1964. They had gained access to the railway cutting through a hole behind Friedrichstrasse station, and were thus able to jump

Escape from West Staaken, Nauen district (GDR), to West Berlin. Five inhabitants of the GDR used a bulldozer to break through the barbed-wire entanglements. GDR border guards are seen here recovering the bulldozer, West Berlin, Spandau district/West Staaken, Finkenkruger Weg, 11 September 1966 (Photo: Landesarchiv Berlin)

on to the international Moscow-Paris express. Prepared cars, bulldozers, heavily laden buses or lorries were repeatedly used for escape attempts. As late as 10 March 1988 three men from the Babelsberg district of Potsdam forced their way through to West Berlin across the Glienicker Bridge in Potsdam.

Although "air" transport provided very few possibilities of escape, it was still used. Thus a Leipzig engineer escaped with his family across the Berlin Wall in summer 1965 using a home-made funicular. The family had previously locked themselves in the toilets of an East Berlin ministerial building. By casting a weighted perlon string from the roof of the building across the border installations, the refugees were able to throw a robust wire rope across the Wall with the help of relatives in West Berlin, who secured it on their side.

In 1978 a young couple from Schafstädt near Merseburg succeeded in escaping in a light aircraft used for agricultural spraying. The husband was an engineer employed in agricultural aviation by Interflug, the GDR state airline. His wife was a dentist. The aircraft succeeded in flying beneath the GDR radar system and after a short flight landed near Bad Lauterberg on the Western side of the Harz mountains. It was not the only escape of its kind.

Among the most spectacular flights (in both senses) from the GDR was one carried out in a balloon by two families from Pössneck in eastern Thuringia in 1979. After the two families had used an old sewing machine to sew together pieces of fabric which they had with great difficulty managed to buy from various sources, a first attempt in the spring of that year failed just short of the border. The abandoned gas-bag and other components were discovered. The Stasi and People's Police started an elaborate search operation in the Gera region. Under the pressure of these events, the families toured 15 GDR towns and cities to buy up material once more, which they finally managed to sew together to make another balloon. The total area of the fabric was 1,250 square metres. In the night of 15/16 September 1976, this home-made hot-air balloon took off from Lobenstein district, the burner being powered by gas from four propane canisters attached to the platform. At times, the balloon reached a height of 2,600 metres. Near the Franconian town of Naila, the bold flight came to a happy end. The escape not only aroused great attention in the media,

Balloon escape: seven out of eight refugees from eastern Thuringia after their successful escape in a home-made hot-air balloon, 1979 (Photo: Frankenpost Hof)

but also became the subject of a film in the USA. One of the last spectacular airborne escapes from the GDR took place in May 1989, just a few months before the Wall came down. Two brothers in West Berlin fetched a third brother out of East Berlin in two home-made aluminium planes. Unnoticed, the aircraft landed in Treptow Park in the East of the city, and equally un-noticed flew back over the Berlin Wall to land in front of the Reichstag building in West Berlin. The aircraft were camouflaged with Soviet markings. A particular chapter in the story of escapes concerns those in which water played a role, in other words across the border rivers – the Elbe, Werra and (in Berlin) the Spree – and of course the Baltic Sea. The border area was already marked five kilometres off the Baltic coast, and was accompanied by security installations. It was guarded by the 6th Border Brigade (Coast), which was under the direct command of the Volksmarine, the "People's Navy". In close co-operation with other "organs" of the GDR, such as the Stasi and the police, there was also in the coastal area a particularly close-meshed web of plain-clothes operatives at work, who not only kept an eye on the local people, but also, and especially, on holidaymakers, amateur sports enthusiasts, and campers.

Car parks, holiday homes and campsites were kept under careful surveillance, and as a result many would-be refugees were already trapped in this web before they had a chance to attempt to cross the water itself. After the building of the Berlin Wall in 1961, more than 5,600 people still sought to cross the border by swimming, diving, paddling, surfing or simply taking a fishing boat across the Baltic Sea. Only 903 refugees actually reached the coast of Schleswig-Holstein, Denmark or Sweden. Between 1961 and 1989, at least 174 people paid for the escape attempt across the Baltic with their lives, most of them through drowning or hypothermia.

4,522 Baltic refugees were caught and in many cases imprisoned for years. Most escape attempts were registered by border guards in the western half of the Bay of Wismar, where the distance from to Schleswig-Holstein, between Boltenhagen and Travemünde, was shortest, although here the border security was particularly tight. The Fischland-Darss peninsula close to the international shipping route and the islands of Rügen and Hiddensee close to the Danish island of Møn also promised good starting points for an escape attempt. It was by swimming, mostly in home-made

Escape via the Baltic – In the Schöneberg sports hall in West Berlin, Bernd Böttger demonstrates how he reached the lightship "Gedser" from Warnemünde using an underwater engine on the night of 8/9 September 1968 (Photo: ullstein bild – dpa)

rubber suits, that more than a third of the would-be refugees sought to reach a Western ship or the coast of West Germany or Denmark, even though this meant covering distances of between 30 and 50 kilometres. The last known successful escape by a swimmer across the Baltic was on 2 September 1989. Just a few weeks before the Wall came down, the young man from Saxony spent 19 hours covering 38 kilometres before he was fished out of the water by the crew of a West German ship.

Numerous technical aids were used by the aquatic refugees too. Doubtless the most spectacular invention was that of Bernd Böttger (1940–1972) from Sebnitz on the Czech border, who brilliantly developed the world's first "Aqua-scooter" powered by a bicycle auxiliary engine. A first unsuccessful attempt ended with eight months in a GDR jail in 1967. With a newly built appliance and diving equipment, Böttger made a second attempt on 8 September 1968. Half a metre under water, the prototype "Aqua-scooter" pulled its inventor through the Baltic at a speed of five kilometres an hour. After almost six hours at sea, navigating by the stars, he was finally picked up by a West German ship. The appliance he used was patented and series-produced by a West German company. The US Navy equipped its combat swimmers with them, and the "Aqua-scooter" built by the amateur inventor from Saxony became world-famous through its appearance in James Bond films.

Almost as soon as a German Border Police force was set up in the Soviet zone, there were repeated desertions of border police officers across the sector and zonal borders. After the establishment of the GDR, desertion by border police or soldiers continued to be a serious problem. The building of the Berlin Wall and the constantly increasing security on the inner-German border made escape more difficult for the service personnel too, but even so, the GDR authorities registered numerous such cases, especially in the 1960s. The photo of the NCO Conrad Schumann (1942–1998) jumping over the barbed wire in Berlin on 15 October 1961 went around the world. Also spectacular was the flight of a group of border soldiers who broke through the Wall in a tank followed by a truck in the Treptow district of Berlin in April 1963.

The introduction of conscription in the GDR in 1962, and the consequent more intensive vetting procedure for planned service on the border, along with the constant surveillance of border guards by official and unofficial Stasi workers, gradually reduced the number of cases of desertion. Even so, by 1989 some 2,800 officers, NCOs and men of the border guards had deserted to the West. In order to prevent possible collaboration on such enterprises, the make-up of shifts was changed on a daily basis. In a few cases there were also escape attempts by members of the Soviet armed forces stationed in the GDR. Knowing that deserters faced the death penalty, these often heavily armed Red Army soldiers were not squeamish when faced with their East German counterparts on the inner-German border. Particularly dramatic were escape attempts

Six refugees used this cable reel to escape from the GDR to West Berlin, January 1965 (Photo: Landesarchiv Berlin)

by GDR citizens where the refugees, wounded by gunfire or mines or spring-guns shortly before reaching the final obstacle, found themselves in an almost hopeless situation. A case which attracted the attention of the world's press took place in December 1971 on a section of the border in the southern Harz region near Brochthausen/Fuhrbach. The event showed up the treacherous nature of the border security to a particular degree. A young married couple with a small child had been stopped by a mine exploding, and the woman had lost both her feet. Her husband was also injured, though less seriously. West German civilians, supported by West German customs officials, managed to haul the refugees through the wire-mesh fence.

"Through our ideological work we must ensure that every member of the border guard is thoroughly convinced that every border violator – in whichever direc-

Berlin Wall, night view of the border installations on Bernauer Strasse, 1986 (Photo: ullstein bild – Ritter)

tion he seeks to break through the border – is an enemy of our republic, or transforms himself into an enemy the moment he defects to the imperialist camp and thus

provides the Ultras with new material for their campaign of hate and slander against our republic. ... The
soldier must be aware that for friends, there are crossing-points on the state borders. Those who seek to cross
the borders of our sovereign state, however ... are enemies and will be treated as enemies. ... To show un-

derstanding for traitors is to act against the interests of the whole people."

Heinz Hoffmann. In: Sozialistische Landesverteidigung. Reden und Aufsätze 1963–1970, Berlin 1971.

The worst chapter in the history of the inner-German border is that concerning the 700 people who lost their lives while seeking to exercise a basic human right, the right of freedom of movement. Even in the immediate post-war period, there were already deaths of refugees on the border of the Soviet zone. The closing of the "green border" in 1952 and finally the building of the Berlin Wall in 1961 with an intensified border regime made escape an undertaking that carried a deadly risk. On 24 August 1961, eleven days after the Berlin border was closed, Günter Litfin (1937–1961) was shot and killed as he tried to cross Humboldt Harbour, and thus became the first fatal casualty of the still inchoate Berlin Wall.

Within the next year, a further 29 refugees were to die on the border between East and West Berlin. Worldwide outrage was triggered above all by the death of Peter Fechter (1944–1962). An 18-year-old building worker, he was shot down in a hail of bullets on 17 August 1962 and seriously wounded. He lay on the ground in front of the Wall on the East German side of the border near the Checkpoint Charlie crossing-point. Crying for help and bleeding to death, he was given no assistance and died hours later beneath the eyes of the GDR border guards, who did nothing, the West Berlin police, American soldiers and an angry crowd in West Berlin, who could only watch helplessly as the young Berliner died a gruesome death on the East Berlin side of the border. Hardly any other event at the Berlin wall so outraged the people of Berlin and indeed the whole world, and of course Western politicians.

Recovery of the body of Günter Litfin, shot dead by GDR border police on 24 August 1961, Humboldt Harbour, Berlin, Mitte district (Photo: Landesarchiv Berlin/Karl-Heinz Schubert)

Shortly after this atrocity, there were numerous protest demonstrations in West Berlin, with both American and Red Army soldiers coming under attack. West Berlin politicians, for example the future Chancellor Willy Brandt, realized that their primary duty must be to make the Wall more permeable, an insight that, embodied in the slogan "Wandlung durch Annäherung" ("Change through Rapprochement") finally became a focus of all West German governments, starting in 1972 with the coalition of Social and Free Democrats.

On the evening of 5 February 1989, 20-year-old Chris Gueffroy (1968–1989) was shot dead at the Berlin Wall, and thus became the last fatal casualty on the inner-German border. International protests forced the GDR leadership to abandon the use of firearms by the border guards. Since the building of the Wall in 1961, 45 people had been killed by mines or spring-guns, and more than 200 shot dead on the inner-German border. Including those who drowned while attempting to escape across the Baltic or inland waterways, plus the 27 border guards who were killed in action, the number of post-1961 fatalities reached almost 700. The number of those injured, in some cases seriously, at the "peace border", to use the GDR jargon, ran into hundreds.

Warning signs on the West German side and in West Berlin pointed to the dangerous nature of the GDR border. Nonetheless, there were repeated attempts to cross the border installations from West to East. Often it was merely a case of over-exuberance on the part of young people who, while they risked their lives, in no sense fell into the category of "aggressive imperialist circles" thought up and propagated by the GDR leadership. In March 1962 a woman from Herzberg in the Harz crossed the still imperfectly secured border from West to East in order to attend the funeral of her husband's grandmother in Branderode in East

When 18-year-old Peter Fechter tried to climb over the Wall to West Berlin in 1962, East German border guards opened fire. Fechter remained lying seriously wounded on the "death strip". In spite of his cries for help, the GDR border guards let him bleed to death. An hour later, his body was carried away by border guards, 17 August 1962 (Photo: ullstein bild – Gadewolt)

Border to East Berlin, Prenzlauer Berg district. Flowers at the place where Hans-Dieter Wesa was shot dead on West Berlin territory, S-Bahn station Bornholmer Strasse, Berlin, Wedding district, 23 August 1962 (Photo: Landesarchiv Berlin/Johann Willa)

Germany. After reporting to the GDR border guards, by whom she was interrogated, her wish – eccentric, in the view of the GDR – was acceded to. She was allowed to attend the funeral. She returned by the same route, after being interrogated once again by border guards and police. Also to be included among the curiosities of West-East border crossings were, from the 1970s on, the "Wall leapers", who sought to climb over the Wall from a variety of motives. The American John Runnings provided a particularly spectacular display in 1986/87 with his actions at and indeed on the Berlin Wall, including a 500-metre balancing-act along its top. He came to no harm, any more than did the 200 young West Berliners who, in the summer of 1988, escaped from the West Berlin police by seeking refuge on East Berlin territory by the side of the Wall, pursuing a cat-and-mouse game with their pursuers. Young punks who fled across the Wall to East Berlin were picked up and returned to the West at the regular crossing points.

Shortly after the hermetic sealing of the inner-German border, and the consequent freeze in relations between the two states, the federal government starting trying to buy the freedom of political prisoners in the GDR. After a contact, mediated by the West German publisher Axel Springer (1925–1987), between the then junior minister at the West German foreign office (and future German president) Karl Carstens and certain East Berlin lawyers, by October 1964 the first 798 political prisoners had been freed and were allowed to travel to the West. By 1989, the West German government had purchased the freedom of 33,755 GDR prisoners in this way. While the price for one prisoner was initially 40,000 deutschmarks, this sum rose later to 100,000 deutschmarks, and in some cases more. Altogether the West German government had spent more than 3.5 billion deutschmarks on this humanitarian service by the time the Wall came down. The GDR leadership con-

Schematic illustration of the border system of the GDR, c. 1975 (Repro: Landesarchiv Berlin)

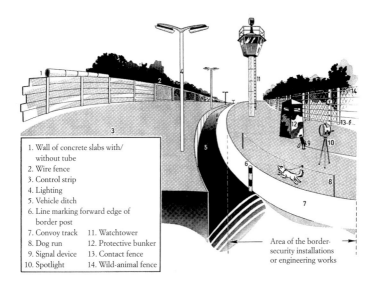

1. Wall of concrete slabs with/ without tube
2. Wire fence
3. Control strip
4. Lighting
5. Vehicle ditch
6. Line marking forward edge of border post
7. Convoy track
8. Dog run
9. Signal device
10. Spotlight
11. Watchtower
12. Protective bunker
13. Contact fence
14. Wild-animal fence

Area of the border-security installations or engineering works

Failed escape on Lindenstrasse (Kreuzberg district): Bernd Sievert is carried away after being shot and wounded, 5 September 1971 (Photo: ullstein bild – Auer)

sciously factored in this inflow of cash to boost its hard-currency reserves.

"As the introduction to the brochure says, human rights have found their home in the GDR. That is a source of pleasure. But we think that in this panorama there is a chapter missing. Why do so many East Germans risk so many dangers in order to leave this "home of human rights"? And why has this country, where freedom blossoms, secured its western border with a Wall whose defenders point their weapons not outwards but inwards? What is missing is a quotation: 'Everyone has the right to leave any country, including his own.' These words are to be found in Article 13 of the Universal Declara-

tion of Human Rights. They are very simple and clear. It would be nice to know what they mean for those exegetes who rule in East Berlin."

Quotation from an article in the Paris newspaper "Combat" on a GDR propaganda brochure intended for foreign distribution, 16 January 1974

With the signing of the CSCE Final Act in Helsinki in 1975, the GDR leadership had undertaken to guarantee its citizens the right of freedom of movement, which included the right to choose where they wanted to live. This led in crucial measure to sections of the GDR population invoking this undertaking and making an application to leave the country. Where family ties played no part, the applicants had mostly decided they wanted nothing more to do with life in the GDR. Responsibility for dealing with these applications lay with the internal affairs department of the relevant local authority.

Initially often dragged out, and also rejected, they still formed in the 1970s a statistically unimportant factor. It was only in the 1980s that the number of such applications became significant, and depending on the period, the great majority were granted. In 1983 more than 6,700 people were "discharged from GDR citizenship" and left for the West, and in the following year almost 30,000 people left the GDR having made the necessary application. By deliberately pushing this wave of emigration, the GDR leadership sought to relieve internal pressure and get rid of opponents of the system. What they achieved was the opposite. The wave of emigration grew stronger, and led ultimately to increased awareness of the problem among large sections of the GDR population. Applying for permanent emigration meant for most applicants a gruelling process that often took years and was accompanied by a number of sometimes burdensome restrictions. Applicants were until well into the 1980s treated as criminals, harassed, intimidated and limited in what jobs they could take.

Loss of an existing job was also a possibility. The applicants came under intense surveillance by the Stasi, while their children were sometimes discriminated against at kindergarten and school. The people involved often lived with their suitcases packed. Some of the would-be emigrants sold all their belongings, while others bought things, hoping to sell them in the West for cash with which to start a new life. Alongside, in some cases, social isolation, many had to live with the risk of breaking East German law if, in order to speed up their applications, they made contact with the missions of the Federal Republic or other Western countries, institutions or individuals. Emigration-applicants ultimately formed a closed group in GDR society, often loosely organized and giving signs by which they could be identified. For those with no family ties, these contacts, along with their friends and relations in the West, sometimes arranged temporary marriages in the GDR between West and East German citizens with a view to speeding up the application. In some cases, when the "marriage of convenience" was later dissolved, the women involved had to cope with serious disadvantages even when they had reached the West.

The run-up to the official departure from the GDR, which ended with the formal document certifying "deprivation of citizenship", and the surrender of identity cards, was, for the applicant, a bureaucratic endurance course. Among other things, they had to declare all goods they wished to take with them. They also had to separately list, for the benefit of local culture departments, all old items, from the crystal vase to the "antique" cupboard. These were vetted by state-appointed assessors, the intention being to prevent the export of the GDR's "cultural heritage". All these visits to the authority came with a price-tag. Once all the hurdles had been taken, emigrants, in the early years of the emigration wave, knew that once they had left, there would be no coming back for a long time. This practice was relaxed by the GDR leadership in the late 1980s. When finally, in the first six months of 1989, more than 46,000 people emigrated following successful application, and the shouts of "We want out!" at the demonstrations starting in autumn of that year grew ever louder, the days of the existence of the inner-German border and thus of the GDR were numbered.

While the number of above all young refugees via Hungary and Czechoslovakia unheard-of heights in 1989, there was in parallel an enormous increase in GDR citizens seeking refuge via the West German embassies in Warsaw, Prague, Budapest and the Permanent Representation of the Federal Republic in East Berlin itself. Already since the 1970s, there had been occasional occupations of West German embassies by GDR citizens seeking to force the authorities to let them emigrate. Thus a group of 160 embassy squatters in Prague in 1984 had their freedom bought by the Federal Interior Ministry. From August 1989, though, the situation got out of hand.

The embassy squats by numerous East Germans led to the closure, because of overcrowding, of the Permanent Representation of the Federal Republic in East Berlin on 8 August, of the West German embassy in Prague on 23 August and of that in Warsaw on 19 September. Even so, more and more would-be emigrants succeeded in gaining access to (especially) the compound of the embassy in Prague. At times, there were up to 4,000 people here, including numerous small children, in conditions that were steadily deteriorating. Negotiations between the two German states, resulted in the emotional appearance of West German Foreign Minister Hans-Dietrich Genscher on the balcony

Illuminated sign in Friedrich- strasse station, East Berlin, Mitte district (Photo: Zeit- geschicht- liches Forum Leipzig)

of the Prague embassy in the early evening of 30 September. His words: "Dear compatriots, we have come here to inform you that today it has become possible for you to emigrate to the Federal Republic" were virtually lost in the cheers from the thousands of embassy squatters. The exodus of the refugees in special trains across the territory of the GDR, demanded by the communist leadership, was one of the last impotent attempts on their part not to lose face. When a train full of emigrants passed through Dresden on 4 October, a few days before the 40th anniversary of the founding of the GDR, there were massive confrontations with the People's Police when young Dresdeners attempted to jump on.

In ever more rapidly succeeding waves, the Prague embassy above all was occupied by thousands of would-be refugees from East Germany wishing to avail themselves of the opportunity which had now opened up. Helpless, the GDR leadership now introduced obligatory visas for travel to Czechoslovakia, a decision revoked once more on 1 November 1989. The renewed pressure of thousands of refugees in Prague finally led to Czechoslovakia's allowing GDR citizens direct access to West Germany from its territory on 3 November 1989.

Within three days, more than 50,000 East Germans had quickly decided to exploit this new possibility of reaching the Federal Republic in uncomplicated fashion. After 1988 had seen the exodus of 39,832 people from the GDR to West Germany, that figure rose to a total of 343,854 in 1989. Of these, more than 120,000 had forced their exit by squatting in the West German embassies in Warsaw, Budapest and Prague.

GDR citizens determined to emigrate take refuge in the grounds of the West German embassy in Prague. Czech police seek to prevent a man climbing the fence. 2 October 1989 (Photo: ullsteinbild – AP)

THE FALL OF THE WALL AND THE END OF THE INNER-GERMAN BORDER 1989/90

The politburo of the SED has *"today decided ... er ... to make an arrangement which will allow any citizen of the GDR ... er ... to leave the country via border crossing-points of the GDR."* *"When does this arrangement come into force? Immediately?"* *"Well, comrades, this is my information: ... private journeys abroad may be applied for without any preconditions such as good cause or family affairs. ... As far as I am aware this is ... with immediate effect."... "Does it apply to West Berlin?" "Well ... yes, yes."*

Günter Schabowski, member of the politburo of the SED and First Secretary of the district committee of the SED in Berlin (GDR), at a press conference, 9 November 1989, during a live TV broadcast

This if anything unspectacular text, doubtless reluctantly delivered, in this form at least, was of world-historical importance, not only bringing down as it did the inner-German border and the Berlin Wall, but causing the East German state to collapse like a house of cards. The precipitate opening of the borders on 9 November 1989, after 28 years with an imprisoned population, had precisely the consequence that the Soviet occupiers and the GDR government, with the SED at its head, had foreseen back in 1961, and was the reason why they had built the Wall in the first place. Their own people now not only had the alternative in front of their eyes, they voted with their feet. The now unstoppable exodus, the internal opposition, which in the late 1980s had increasingly been emerging from church circles, and the huge (and getting huger by the week) in the autumn of 1989, paralysed a party and state leadership which was no longer in control of events and had only limited scope for reaction. The economic decline of the GDR had, as in the Soviet Union and eastern Europe generally, so weakened the strength of the communist bloc that nothing was any longer possible without the help of the "class enemy" in the Federal Republic and Western Europe. Only a few hours before the Wall came down, the GDR leadership had, for the umpteenth time, requested loans to the tune of billions of deutschmarks from West Germany. It is one of the curiosities of German history that the billions already granted had not only somewhat prolonged the death throes of the GDR but had also kept alive the immense military apparatus along with a gigantic surveillance system and not least the inner-German border.

ADN (the official GDR news agency), radio stations, the "Aktuelle Kamera" news that went out on GDR television at 7.30 pm, and finally the West German primetime TV news programme, the "Tagesschau" at 8.00 pm, all broadcast the announcement of the imminent opening of the border, and the news spread like wildfire. By 8.30 pm, hundreds of people had gathered on the East Berlin side of the Bornholmer Strasse crossing point. The first West Berliners likewise assembled at various crossing-points in order to see if the news was really true. Finally, under the pressure of events, the duty officer at the Bornholmer Strasse crossing point opened the border to West Berlin at 10.30 pm. Neither the border guards nor the Stasi had had any orders from above. The officers of the border guard, completely in the dark about what was going on, used their own judgement. By shortly after midnight, all the border crossings in Berlin were open, and the city was immersed in an indescribable euphoria; almost all the inhabitants were out on the street celebrating. Many could hardly believe it: an inhuman border regime that had come to be seen as al-

Berlin, Bornholmer Strasse crossing-point, 10 November 1989 (Photo: Bundesarchiv Koblenz, 183-1989-1118-018)

most normal had suddenly collapsed. The speech-lessness affected not only the great majority of GDR citizens who had suffered as a result of the Wall, but also that small group who believed the border closure and the Wall had been legitimate measures. It is true that shortly after midnight the GDR border troops were put on heightened combat readiness, while operational committees were formed and other emergency measures were taken by a new GDR leadership, which itself had only been in place for a few days, or in some cases a few hours. But these measures were largely unnoticed and in any case ignored. From the early morning of 10 November millions of GDR citizens could also pass through the crossing-points on the inner-German border, and amidst scenes of joy experienced the same hospitality and readiness to help on the part of their West German compatriots as the Berliners had done a few hours earlier. Very quickly, the "Trabbi", the East German automobile, became a familiar sight on the streets of West Germany and West Berlin. On the evening of 10 November, the West German chancellor, Helmut Kohl, had interrupted an official visit to Poland in order to address a rally outside the Schöneberg Town Hall in West Berlin, together with his foreign minister Hans-Dietrich Genscher, the ruling mayor of West Berlin, Walter Momper, and the honorary chairman of the Social Democratic Party and former chancellor Willy Brandt. It was on this occasion that Brandt, who had for many years held the post of ruling mayor of West Berlin himself, used the later oft-quoted words: "What belongs together is now growing together."

The order issued by the GDR defence minister on 21 December 1989, namely that "border violators" were to be arrested, had long been overtaken by reality. It is true, however, that this order specifically excluded the use of firearms, and also definitively put an end to any strengthening of the border. But in the meantime, border guards had already started dismantling the barriers. In what had previously been an impenetrable border, new crossing-points were opened up. General passport controls, and the attempt to use a new customs law to prevent a "sell-out" of the GDR, constituted the main work of the East German border guards and customs officials until the first half of 1990. The Brandenburg Gate in the heart of Berlin was re-opened to pedestrians on 22 December 1989, and it was here, at this symbol of 28 years of division, that hundreds of thousands of Berliners and their guests saw in the New Year. Already from Christmas Eve, West Germans and West Berliners had been able to visit East Germany and East Berlin without a visa and without the previously compulsory purchase of East German currency. Many million GDR citizens, often waiting in queues

Border with East Berlin. Brandenburg Gate after the lifting of travel restrictions for GDR citizens on the night of 9/10 November 1989. People from the GDR, West Berlin and West Germany at and on the Wall, 10 November 1989 (Photo above: Landesarchiv Berlin/Edmund Kasparski; photo below: Landesarchiv Berlin/Wolfgang Albrecht)

Hirschberg/Rudolphstein crossing point on the A9 Berlin to Nuremberg autobahn, Thuringia/Bavaria, 10 November 1989 (Photo: Bundesarchiv Koblenz, 183-1989-1110-031)

Tailback on the autobahn from Berlin to Hamburg approaching the Zarrentin crossing point, 11 November 1989 (Photo: Bundesarchiv Koblenz, 183-1989-1112-009)

Brandenburg Gate, New Year celebrations, Berlin, Mitte district, 1 January 1990 (Photo: Bundesarchiv Koblenz/ZB Hartmut Reiche, 183-1990-0101-008)

stretching for kilometres, or in overcrowded trains, had meanwhile visited the Western half of Germany, still receiving the customary "welcome money" from local authorities. Traffic routes that had been cut by the border started to be re-opened, while contacts and projects between West and East at local-authority level were set in motion. Border soldiers, customs officers and representatives of other military units on both sides of the border paid each other visits and learned how to speak to each other once more. At the beginning of January, the GDR government, now headed by Prime Minister Hans Modrow, ordered the phased reduction of the GDR border troops by 50% to 25,000 men. The historic development which had begun on 9 November 1989 now took on a dynamism of its own, so rapid that events became hard to keep track of. Given the precipitate changes in the GDR, and under the pressure of a still huge inflow of people from the East, the "German Unity" cabinet committee chaired by Chancellor Kohl was set up on 7 February 1990. In this connexion, Kohl proposed talks with the GDR on a currency union, dependent on economic reform. On 10 February 1990, the Federal Government, on the occasion of an official visit by the chancellor to the Soviet Union, received an assurance from the latter that it would not oppose German re-unification. On 14 March, representatives of both German states, and of the four victors of the Second World War, met in the West German capital Bonn for preliminary talks. This, and subsequent negotiations to which Poland was also invited, has gone down in history as the "Two-plus-four negotiations". In order to stop the continuing mass exodus from the GDR, the federal government resolved to abolish the emergency reception procedure for émigrés from the GDR as from 1 July 1990. On 18 May 1990, the finance ministers of the two German states, in the presence of Chancellor Kohl and the new GDR Prime Minister Lothar de Maizière (a Christian Democrat) signed the State Treaty on currency, economic and social union between the Federal Republic and the GDR. This came into force on 1 July. In

Demolishing the Berlin Wall, Mitte district, summer 1990 (Photo: Wolfgang Kramer)

Demolishing the Berlin Wall, Mitte district, summer 1990 (Photo: Wolfgang Kramer)

Street traders with souvenirs of the Berlin Wall, the GDR, and the Soviet occupation, Berlin, Mitte district, summer 1990 (Photo: Wolfgang Kramer)

advance of the currency and social union, the abolition of controls on the inner-German and Berlin borders was announced on 26 June, and these controls ceased with effect from 1 July. Since January, the GDR had been laboriously dismantling the border installations. The decision, taken by the GDR Council of Ministers, was largely implemented by the GDR border guards. The Berlin Wall, that particular symbol of fear, was destined to have largely disappeared from the face of the city by 30 November 1990.

The numerous "wallpeckers" had already, since the end of 1989, been helping themselves to chunks, and in many cases carried on a thriving souvenir business. Further pieces of the Berlin Wall, big and small, were sent as gifts to personalities, institutions and organizations all over the world, while others were sold. Most of the Wall and of the border installations were broken up and largely used as hardcore in road-building. Just a few historic souvenir sections found

Part of the Berlin Wall in Berlin, Mitte district, which was visited by "wallpeckers", spring 1990 (Photo: Wolfgang Kramer)

their way into museums or memorials. The Treaty on the Creation of German Unity was signed in East Berlin on 31 July 1990 and 3 October designated as the new German National Day. On 21 September 1990, two weeks before re-unification, the GDR minister of disarmament and defence announced the dissolution of the border guards. With the unification of the GDR and the Federal Republic on 3 October 1990, the post-war history of divided Germany, came to a peaceful end, an end hoped for by millions in East and West, but already written off by many. What remained were millions of disrupted lives, but also the knowledge that these changes had been brought about by the people themselves.

LITERATURE

Arbeitsgemeinschaft der Museen, Gedenkstätten und Denkmale an der ehemaligen innerdeutschen Grenze (ed.): Grenzmuseen. Museen, Gedenkstätten und Denkmale an der ehemaligen innerdeutschen Grenze, Töpen-Mödlareuth 1998.

Wolfgang Benz: Deutschland seit 1945. Entwicklungen in der Bundesrepublik und in der DDR. Chronik Dokumente Bilder. Sonderausgabe der Bundeszentrale für politische Bildung, Munich 1990.

Camphausen, Bahr, Schneider: Eine Stadt wächst zusammen. 10 Jahre Deutsche Einheit: Was aus der Berliner Mauer wurde, Berlin 1999.

Thomas Flemming/Hagen Koch: Die Berliner Mauer. Geschichte eines politischen Bauwerkes, Berlin-Brandenburg 2004.

Jutta Gladen: „Man lebt sich auseinander" Von den Schwierigkeiten, Verwandte drüben zu besuchen. Reihe Sachbeiträge. Die Landesbeauftragte für Unterlagen des Staatssicherheitsdienstes der ehemaligen DDR in Sachsen-Anhalt, Magdeburg 2001.

Roman Grafe: Die Grenze durch Deutschland. Eine Chronik von 1945 bis 1990, Berlin 2002.

Grenzlandmuseum Eichsfeld e.V. (ed.): Grenze – mitten in Deutschland. Companion volume to the exhibition in the Grenzlandmuseum Eichsfeld. Schriftenreihe der Bildungsstätte und des Grenzlandmuseums Eichsfeld, vol. 2002.

Horst Gundlach (ed.): Die innerdeutsche Grenze im Südharz. Schicksale – Erlebnisse – Ereignisse, Bad Sachsa 2004.

Handbuch für den Grenzdienst, 6th ed. Berlin 1987.

Ingolf Hermann: Die Deutsch-Deutsche Grenze. Eine Dokumentation. Von Posseck bis Lehesten, von Ludwigstadt nach Prex. 4th ed., Plauen 2001.

Ingolf Hermann/Karsten Sroka: Deutsch-Deutsches Grenzlexikon. Der Eiserne Vorhang und die Mauer in Stichworten. Bürgerkomitee des Landes Thüringen e.V. 2005.

Martin Hürlimann: Berlin Königsresidenz Reichshauptstadt Neubeginn, Zurich/Freiburg i.B. 1981.

Bernd Kuhlmann: Deutsch-Deutsche Grenzbahnhöfe. 2nd ed., Munich 2006.

Volker Koop: Ausgegrenzt. Der Fall der DDR-Grenztruppen, Berlin 1993.

Robert Lebegern: Mauer, Zaun und Stacheldraht: Sperranlagen an der innerdeutschen Grenze 1945–1990, Weiden 2002.

Ulrich Mähler: Kleine Geschichte der DDR. 5th ed., Munich 2007.

Joachim Nawrocki: Bewaffnete Organe in der DDR, Berlin 1979.

Stiftung Haus der Geschichte der Bundesrepublik Deutschland

Zeitgeschichtliches Forum Leipzig (ed.): drüben. Deutsche Blick-wechsel, Leipzig 2006.

Stiftung Haus der Geschichte der Bundesrepublik Deutschland Zeitgeschichtliches Forum Leipzig (ed.): Einsichten. Diktatur und Widerstand in der DDR, Leipzig 2001.

Klaus Hartwig Stoll: Point Alpha. Brennpunkt der Geschichte, Petersberg 2007.

Verein Berliner Mauer – Gedenkstätte und Dokumentationszentrum (ed.): Die Berliner Mauer. Exhibition catalogue Dokumentationszentrum Berliner Mauer, Berlin 2001.

Christine Voigt-Müller: Hinter dem Horizont liegt die Freiheit ... Flucht über die Ostsee, Bielefeld 2004.

Wörterbuch zur Deutschen Militärgeschichte. Schriften des Militärgeschichtlichen Instituts der Deutschen Demokratische Republik, 2nd ed. 1985.

Stefan Wolle: Die heile Welt der Diktatur. Alltag und Herrschaft in der DDR, Berlin 1998.

Rudolf Zietz: Erlebnisse an der Grenze im Harz. Ein Zollbeamter erinnert sich, Duderstadt 2003.

MUSEUMS AND MEMORIALS

Asbach/Sickenberg
Grenzmuseum "Schifflers-
grund" (Border Museum)
37318 Asbach/Sickenberg

Berlin-Kreuzberg
Museum Haus am
Checkpoint Charlie
Friedrichstrasse 43–45
10969 Berlin

Berlin-Mitte
Deutsches Historisches
Museum (Museum of
German History)
Unter den Linden 2
10117 Berlin

Berlin-Mitte
"Parlament der Bäume"
("Parliament of Trees":
Memorial to the victims of the
Berlin Wall)
Schiffbauerdamm between
Marschallbrücke and Kron-
prinzenbrücke (near Reichstag)

Berlin-Wedding
Berlin Wall Memorial
Bernauer Strasse 111
13355 Berlin

Berlin-Zehlendorf
Alliierten-Museum
(Allied Museum)
Clayallee 135 Outpost
14195 Berlin

Dresden
Militärhistorisches Museum
der Bundeswehr (Museum of
Modern Military History)
Olbrichtplatz 2
01099 Dresden

Geisa (Rhön)
Memorial and Educational
Centre "Point Alpha"
Grenzmuseum Rhön
(Border Museum Rhön)
Platz der Deutschen Einheit 1
36419 Geisa

Helmstedt
Zonengrenzmuseum
(Zonal Border Museum)
Südertor 6
38350 Helmstedt

Hötensleben
Grenzdenkmal
(Border Memorial)
Schöninger Strasse
39393 Hötensleben

Kleinmachnow
Checkpoint Bravo e.V.
Waldwinkel 37
14532 Kleinmachnow

Kronach
Memorial Heinersdorf-
Welitsch/Memorial Probst-
zella-Ludwigstadt
Blüterstrasse 18
96317 Kronach

Kühlungsborn
Grenzturm e.V.
(Border Watchtower)
Ostseeallee 19
18225 Kühlungsborn

Leipzig
Museum in der "Runden Ecke"
with Museum im Stasi-Bunker
Dittrichring 24
PF 100345
04003 Leipzig

Leipzig
Stiftung Haus der Geschichte
der Bundesrepublik
Deutschland
Zeitgeschichtliches Forum
Leipzig
Grimmaische Str. 6
04109 Leipzig

Marienborn
Gedenkstätte Deutsche Teilung
(Divided Germany Memorial)
On Autobahn A 2
39365 Marienborn

Mattierzoll
Gedenkstätte Grenze
(Border Memorial)
Schulstrasse
38170 Winnigstedt

Neustadt bei Coburg
Information Centre on Divided
Germany
Georg-Langbein-Strasse 1
96465 Neustadt bei Coburg

Philippsthal (Werra)
Grenzmuseum
(Border Museum)
Schloss 6
36269 Philippsthal

Schnackenburg
Grenzlandmuseum
(Border Territories Museum)
Am Markt 4
29493 Schnackenburg

Schnega
Grenzlandmuseum
(Border Territories Museum)
Göhr Nr. 13
29465 Schnega

Sorge
Freiland-Grenzmuseum
(Open-air Border Museum)
Sorge
Förstenbergstrasse 3
38875 Sorge

Tann
Information Centre on the
Border and the former GDR
Am Kalkofen 6
36142 Tann (Rhön)

Teistungen
Grenzlandmuseum
(Border Territories Museum)
Eichsfeld
Duderstädter Strasse 5
37339 Teistungen

Töpen-Mödlareuth
Deutsch-Deutsches Museum
(German-German Museum)
Mödlareuth 13
95183 Töpen

Michael Imhof and
León Krempel

BERLIN
New Architecture
A guide to the new
buildings from 1989
to today

16,5 x 24 cm, 160 pages
390 colour images
Paperback
ISBN 978-3-935590-15-0
12.80 €

Paul Wietzorek

HISTORIC BERLIN

17 x 17 cm, 192 pages
190 illustrations
Hardcover
ISBN 978-3-86568-353-3
9.95 €

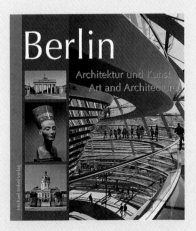

Michael Imhof

BERLIN
Architektur und Kunst
Art and Architecture

22 x 25 cm, 160 pages
308 colour images
Hardcover
text: German/English
ISBN 978-3-86568-100-3
14.95 €